sour grapes

Cellar notes of a wine amateur

Neil Pendock

TAFELBERG

First edition in 2008 by
Tafelberg
An imprint of NB Publishers, 40 Heerengracht, Cape Town 8001

First edition, first impression 2008

Publisher: ANSIE KAMFFER
Editor: MARK RONAN
Proofreader: LOUISE STEYN
Indexer: ANNA TANNEBERGER
Design: ANTON SASSENBERG
Photographer: SIMONÉ SCHOLTZ

Printed and bound by: Paarl Print, Oosterland Street, Paarl, South Africa

ISBN-10: 0-624-04613-3
ISBN-13: 978-0-624-04613-4

Preface

Wine is much more than an alcoholic beverage – it's a cultural reliquary, a liquid time machine that can instantly transport the drinker back to summers long lost quicker than Proust's *madeleine*. People and stories make wine special and the South African Winelands provide some of the most beautiful locations in which they play out.

The idea for this slim volume was spawned at the 2007 Cape Town Book Fair when Tafelberg publishers commissioned this book. I was part of a panel discussion on the crisis (or otherwise) in South African wine chaired by former *Sunday Times* columnist David Bullard.

Some of the text has appeared before in edited form – in the *Sunday Times*, *Financial Mail*, *WINE*, *Winescape*, *Good Taste*, www.winenews.co.za, in my blog, blogs.thetimes.co.za/pendock – and some I wrote especially for this book at the Ouro Minas Palace Hotel in Belo Horizonte between September and November 2007.

This is the result: the inside story on South African wine.

Contents

Introduction

'Listen, all you need to take is a lipstick
and I two bottles of wine'

(BREYTEN BREYTENBACH, *In a Cab in the Rain, New York*)

Kitchen potboilers are suddenly in season: Marco Pierre White spilt much more than the beans in *White Slave* (Orion, 2006), while Anthony Bourdain didn't disappoint with *The Nasty Bits* (Blooms-bury, 2006). My favourite was *Heat* (Knopf, 2006) by Bill Buford and the subtitle explains why: 'An amateur's adventures as kitchen slave, line cook, pasta-maker and apprentice to a Dante-quoting butcher in Tuscany.'

For Bill, whose day job is writing for *The New Yorker*, can certain-ly write and he's a true amateur in the original sense of the word – someone who does it for love.

In South Africa, so-called professionals, self-appointed bibu-lous boffins, sacred cows, or moos (*m*asters *o*f *o*lfactory *s*ubjects they never taught you at university) and wine insiders attempt to achieve status by putting down amateurs and the result is as obvi-ous as a wine lake or a *muf* bottle of Crouchen Blanc. From serious side effects, like South African wine consumption on a relentless downward spiral, to fear of ordering wine in a restaurant in case of committing a social faux pas, snobbishness about wine is silly and suburban.

Far too many South African commentators are alternately bark-ers and shills or paid purveyors of PR-speak, the lingua franca of a profession described by *Sunday Times* restaurant reviewer, AA Gill, ('Britain's most waspish and possibly best-paid critic', according to *The Guardian)* as 'the headlice of civilisation'. But perhaps even worse, they're usually pompous and boring.

A couple of years ago, Nederburg came up with an initiative to make a blended wine to be sold at the annual Nederburg Auction, with the proceeds nobly given to charity. The name of the blend was Nederburg Amateur, recognising the passion that wine lovers feel for the fermented fruit of the vine. While the Fourth Estate assembled the blend, in this case a more worthy constituency would have been people who drink wine and even pay for it themselves, like the members of the 50 wine clubs who enter the annual Blaauwklippen Blending Competition, now in its third decade. The 2006 winning red blend was made by Amanda de Vos of the Knysna Wynproe gilde, while the 2007 was assembled by Roland Frost from the Symposia Wine Society in Durban, who, refreshingly, 'just threw the Cabernet and Malbec together in equal proportions to get 70 per cent and then added the Shiraz and Cabernet Franc'.

When it comes to writing about the fermented fruit of the vine, amateurs certainly have a clear edge over the pros. One of America's hippest novelists, Jay McInerney, is also her finest wine writer. Online lifestyle magazine *Salon.com* calls him 'the best wine writer in America'. The author of the novel that nailed the hedonistic excesses of eighties Manhattan, *Bright Lights, Big City*, latterly turned wine columnist for *House & Garden*, is more bashful. Jay describes himself as 'a passionate amateur' who employs 'a metaphoric language' in comparing wines to 'actresses, rock bands, pop songs, painters or automobiles', rather than a 'literal parsing of scents and tastes' à la Platter's, the wine guide that annually features in the list of South African non-fiction best-sellers.

Jayspeak has a definite louche flair, dating back to his days as a cocaine novelist from the Reagan era. Take his definition of Botrytis, the beneficial fungus that desiccates grapes and produces the concentrated marvels of Sauternes: 'Not since Baudelaire smoked opium has corruption resulted in such beauty.' Or his rule of thumb for separating Burgundy from Bordeaux: 'If it's red, French, costs too much, and tastes like the water that's left in the vase after the flowers have died and rotted, it's probably Burgundy.'

South Africa's own Burgundy boffin, Anthony Hamilton Russell, recounts Jay cooking him and his wife a perfect steak in his Manhattan apartment, with F. Scott Fitzgerald's desk in the study, a present from one of his many wives. Which is quite appropriate, given that Jay McInerney could be mistaken for Jay Gatsby, the hero of Fitzgerald's masterpiece, *The Great Gatsby*, as a result of his sharp dressing and hedonistic lifestyle, flying around the world to eat medieval Kyoto cuisine paired with vintage Dom Pérignon. And in his documentation of the fashionable edge, McInerney is the F. Scott Fitzgerald *de nos jours*.

Even the wine professionals think he's great, with America's über-palate, Robert Parker, calling him 'brilliant, witty, comical and often shamelessly candid and provocative'.

Jay's own winespeak hero and role model is the late Auberon Waugh, who'd certainly get my vote for best wine writer of the last millennium. His comment on the perils of being a wine hack supplies reason enough:

> 'Wine writing should be camped-up. The writer should never like a wine; he should be in love with it; never find a wine disappointing but identify it as a mortal enemy, an attempt to poison him; sulphuric acid should be discovered when there is the faintest hint of sharpness. Bizarre and improbable side tastes should be proclaimed: mushrooms, rotting wood, black treacle, burned pencils, condensed milk, sewage, the smell of French railway stations or ladies' underwear.'

After all, what would you rather hear over dinner – the ghost of Auberon ('Red, I should say. And very nice.') or a discussion on whether that spicy character that everyone enjoyed 'had notes of Brett or Geosmin' (think 'beetroot')?

What follows is my attempt at an amateur's overview of South African wine: opinionated, outrageous and over the top. Cheers!

Connoisseurs

The Sunday Times Lifestyle *supplement ran a short-lived column, 'Typecast', taking the piss out of social stereotypes. Wine snobs are deserving targets, as my contribution set out to confirm.*

'Our palates have moved on', is the cry of the lesser-spotted wine anorak bearing down on the Afrodisiac Restaurant and Voodoo Lounge, their bottles of French in the Alessi Chiringuito wine tote bag complete with mobile phone holder.

'You see, South African cuvées lack the linearity of flavours you find in claret.'

Usually found in pairs – an audience is an important component of wine appreciation – wine anoraks can be identified at one hundred paces by all the stuff they bring with them.

In addition to the Alessi Chiringuito wine tote, there's the enormous bespoke bubinga box (that's African rosewood for the rest of us) for the Riedel glassware (motto: wine tastes better in glasses bigger than your head). Then there's the compulsory handcrafted Château Laguiole corkscrew (wine opener, as it's called for a more effete effect), its black horn handle signed by Enrico Bernardo ('best sommelier in the world, 2004'), nestling like a joey in a leather pouch attached to the Gharani Strok belt.

Unpacking makes an amusing floorshow for other diners, as an array of bizarrely shaped glasses are revealed – different designs for non-vintage and vintage champagne, sparkling versus still mineral water, etc. After a deft final polish with the chamois and a cautionary sniff of the empty glass, they're off.

To start, something outlandish like a biodynamic oak-fermented champagne from Jacques Selosse of Avize ('visits strictly by appointment and please only by those with a serious interest in biodynamic and organic wines'), described in Philippe Boucheron's indispensable travel guide, *Destination Champagne*, (Wine Destination, 2005) as strictly for serious wine geeks. Bollinger's ungrafted pre-phyl-loxera fizz, Vieilles Vignes Françaises, is no longer an option, after all that product placement in James Bond films.

And it has to be champagne: the bubbles of local sparkling wine are far too coarse for the refined lingual papillae of a wine anorak. After the bubbly, it's carefully away with the crystal flutes and out with the white. Probably a Riesling, a varietal loved by anoraks (and hardly anyone else), with a Riesling Revival punted nearly as often as a Rosé Renaissance by wine magazines that can't let an alliteration go unpublished. A Riesling preferably from Alsace; however, now that pre-war German nobility is making a bid to return to the heights of society by making wine, something from the Pfalz might do, so long as it's at least a Spätlese Trocken.

What a pity they don't drink South African, as a German baron is now making a Bordeaux blend in Philadelphia (Western Cape), using a winemaker who's a count. Truman Capote would have swooned. So it'll have to be claret. Château Lynch Bages (Pauillac) perhaps (or maybe not: English wine anoraks disrespectfully call it 'Lunch Bags'). Or Château Pavie (St-Emilion) 2003. It doesn't matter that it's so concentrated as to be almost undrinkable. Robert Parker scores it 95–100 points.

All this whetted my thirst to take the whole matter of connois-seurship a bit further.

Don Quixote was the first modern novel, so no surprise that Miguel de Cervantes chose an enduring theme that has been popular right up to *Bridget Jones's Diary* – ridiculous failure. No surprise either that the Man from La Mancha proclaimed himself an ace wine taster:

> 'Let me smell one and I can tell positively its country, its kind, its flavour and soundness, the changes it will undergo and everything that appertains to it.'

Wine expertise is often a well-established bluff, akin to dexterity with crystal balls or agility with tarot cards. As Steve Shapin, Professor of the History of Science at Harvard, put it in the *London Review of Books:*

> 'Common sense has always suspected that connoisseurship was just snobbery tricked out as expertise, and that wine connoisseurship was one of the purest forms of pretence.'

Removing wine pundits from the sort of pedestals that contemplative monks like St Simeon Stylites used to erect is a deeply felt democratic urge. The website www.winedemocracy.com proclaims:

> 'The most effective way to restrict democracy is to transfer decision making from the public arena to unaccountable institutions: kings and princes, party dictatorships, or professional wine critics.'

A compendium of wine reviews submitted by e-mail, Winedemocracy is a do-it-yourself Platter's with a couple of benefits: potentially more up to date, certainly cheaper and with no obvious conflicts of interest, which sabotage the hard copy Platter's (the taster who rated the estate from which she sources grapes for her own brand; the producer-tasters who rate their competition sighted; the taster who wears a retailer's smock under his anorak; the taster who doubles as a highly paid consultant to several wineries and is chairman of a major producer, and the taster who will come and rate your wine and tell you where you're going wrong, for an obscenely large fee).

Not too many South African entries in Winedemocracy yet, but let's hope it doesn't become the wine world's equivalent of Amazon. com, where book reviews in the form of the most over-the-top gushes are often sent in by the authors themselves under assumed names.

The late philosopher Susan Sontag was not wrong when she noted that 'taste has no system and no proofs'. Nowhere is her point made more sharply than in the results of South African wine competitions. While only a pedant would expect total consistency between shows, at least broad trends should be preserved. Not so. While, in 2006, *WINE* acclaimed a record number of five-star wines (seven as opposed to a ten-year annual average of 2.3), Platter's recorded an all-time low: only 11 five-star stunners, down from 17 the previous year, which makes you wonder if the pundits were tasting the same wines. Or, perhaps, did monkeys do the selection? (See appendix.)

Lawrence Osborne, author of *The Accidental Connoisseur* (North Point Press, 2004), could have had Sontag in mind when he told *The New York Sun* he's really not a wine writer. He's actually into norms: 'My real subject is the creation of norms, inside ourselves, I mean, not outside.' Just like those proposed by wine competitions, perhaps.

Proofs aside, Sontag did detect 'something like a logic of taste: the consistent sensibility which underlies and gives rise to a certain taste'. But then it's unlikely she had South African wine competitions in mind, which are typically run for profit by people trying to sell the stuff or advertising space in magazines – the equivalent of foxes guarding chicken coops. Even features are tarnished when the advertising department calls asking if you'd like to place an ad, as the reporter will be doing a survey story on your Bovlei appellation. No pressure.

As *Financial Times* columnist Patrick Marmion reminded us on the eve of the Academy Awards:

> 'In an age of cultural relativism, the creations of pantheons of perceived excellence consecrated by televised ceremonies may be all we can agree on. If so, artificially created league tables must not be allowed to slough off their manmade character, lest they be mistaken for truth.'

But when it's the TV celebrity who puts in the boot, you've got a real problem. Like design guru Sir Terence Conran (his dad, Gerry, came from East London), who massacred South African haute cuisine and Carrol Boyes cutlery when he attended a Cape Town Design Indaba with glamorous wife, Lady Vicki. Or the Clarkson crash …

INAPPROPRIATE ONES

Connoisseurs fall naturally into three categories: the inappropriate, the accidental and the genuine. Nothing spins the bow ties of wine snobs faster than when 'unqualified' palates dare to pass comment. Something that happened with bells on when Jezzer roared into town.

Sunny Cape Town is a popular destination for British journos during the UK winter, when living in London has all the charm of a dirty, wet lettuce. Which explains the annual summer migration of opinion formers and hacks down south. Jaguar jetted motoring journos to the Winelands in February 2006 as part of a 53-day global launch of the XK Convertible. In April, Wines of South Africa (WOSA, the exporters' association) decanted the wine press into the Convention Centre for Cape Wine 2006, the biannual industry show and tastefest.

Alas for WOSA, Jeremy Clarkson, the most famous petrolhead of them all, had rubbished South African wine in a review published in the *Sunday Times* the previous month. *The Sun* and *Sunday Times* car columnist, outspoken author and presenter of BBC2 motoring programme *Top Gear* (which boasts 350 million viewers worldwide), Clarkson is to car journalism what Robert Parker is to wine rating, Oprah Winfrey is to book reviews or Adamastor is to sea monsters.

Clarkson was billeted in the luxurious Lanzerac Hotel in Stellenbosch, and an evening tour of the estate cellar was laid on for him and his wife. The result: a PR pile-up, when Clarkson described the all-singing, all-dancing Lanzerac cellar as:

'Full of huge steel vats and pressure gauges. It was like being in a nuclear power station' with the end result 'pretty much like the stuff that comes from the outlet pipe at Sellafield [a nuclear power station in the northwest of England]. I doubt the French would put it in their windscreen-washer bottles.'

Lanzerac becomes a symbol for South African wine and Jezzer develops his antipathy into a theme running right through the story. On the evidence of one evening's tasting, South African wine is given the flick: 'You certainly don't go to South Africa for the viniculture.'

We shouldn't be too surprised; after all, Clarkson is no stranger to xenophobic controversy. As *Wikipedia* records, at the Birmingham Motor Show, he claimed the people working on the Hyundai stand had eaten a dog and that the designer of the Hyundai XG had probably had a spaniel for his lunch. German fan belts last 1,000 years (a reference to Hitler and his 1,000-year Reich), while his reaction to the slow response in the aftermath of Hurricane Katrina was: 'Most Americans barely have the brains to walk on their back legs.'

And yet, by his own admission, Clarkson is no wine expert. He once noted in a review:

'When you're out for dinner, why does the waiter invite you to taste the wine? Why doesn't he do it himself? He's the expert and as a general rule most customers would struggle to tell the difference between a 1945 Château Pétrus and a glass of Ribena. I certainly fall into this category. I know nothing about viniculture and, having smoked half a million Marlboros, have no taste buds either. You could pee in a glass and if it were chilled enough I'd be happy.'

Which, nonetheless, didn't stop him trashing Lanzerac and, by extension, South African wine. His smoking habit rings true. He was expelled from his English public school, Repton (founded in 1557), 'for drinking and smoking', before going on to sell Paddington Bear toys for his parents and, from there, to journalism.

Not that he's by any stretch a gastronomic ignoramus, having claimed to have eaten seal flipper, which tasted 'exactly like licking a hot Turkish urinal'. He's also tried whale, which 'tastes like steak, but with an iron tang'.

'The waiter asked if I wanted some grated puffin on my whale and how do you say no to something like that?' Which all sounds a bit like a Monty Python sketch.

However, Clarkson draws the line at turtle: 'I've eaten snakes, dogs, small, whole birds in France and crocodiles, but Tommy Turtle is my line in the sand. I don't care if turtles turn out to be the antidote for cancer, I'm not eating even a small part of one and that's that.'

When it comes to buying wine, Jezzer offers a few tips: 'For home consumption I have two very simple rules designed to make sure my guests don't spend the night driving the porcelain bus. I never spend less than £10 on a bottle, and I only buy stuff that's French.' Which rules out South African on both counts, with most Cape cuvées languishing at the £3.99 level in the UK.

South Africa, though, is not the only wine producer to get the Clarkson treatment:

> 'I'm told the Bulgarians make a decent drop these days, but I imagine that they also make a lot of rubbish. And how are you supposed to know which is which? Which will take you out with the immediacy of a poisoned umbrella and which will be like angels copulating on your tongue? Maybe wine should come with press cuttings on the label, such as you find outside a West-End theatre: "An absolute corker" (Oz Clarke). "I'd rather lick a monkey's nostril" (Jilly Goolden).'

That said, pundits are not the complete solution, since they:

' . . . talk in a language that nobody understands. You think torque and scuttle-shake are a dark art? I once heard Goolden say that one wine tasted like "hot handbags in a Bovril factory". Is that a good thing? Anyway, because of this wine minefield, I always breeze past the offerings from Uruguay and Tibet and buy only French. In the same way that people who know nothing about cars only buy BMWs. There's a sense you can't go too far wrong.'

Recent developments, however, might spoil his love affair with *le vin français*:

'Now, though, it seems like my simple and rather brilliant plan is to be wrecked, because Australia recently overtook France as the biggest wine supplier to Britain and the French have decided to fight back by making Aussie-style, easy-on-the-palate, industrialised global plonk.'

An observation confirmed by the news that French authorities are to permit the use of oak chips as a wine-flavouring additive and sanction the use of the Australian spinning cone to reduce alcohol levels. In addition, the names of grape cultivars are to be permitted on the labels of wines classified as *vin de pays* and above.

Clarkson, who is something of an old fogey at heart, is not well pleased:

'This move has traditionalists in France in a state of high dudgeon, and I'm not surprised. For them it's the thin end of the wedge, an Anglo-Saxon free-market hammer blow to their subsidised villagey way of life. For these people, with their berets and their pre-war tractors, wine should speak of its origins and taste of the soil in which it was grown. And who cares if no one actually buys it. I have no idea what they're talking about, of course. If I tried a wine that tasted

of soil I'd send it back straight away. But I know what they
mean and they're right.'

British Sunday newspapers have a habit of sending inappropriate
celebrities to South Africa to report on wine. The *Sunday Telegraph*
did it a couple of years ago when they packed former England
cricket captain David Gower off on a wine tour with their wine
pundit, Robert Joseph. Tasting at Meerlust, Gower opined: 'If
anyone catches me trying to buy this wine, will they please shoot
me?' of his host's Chardonnay 1999, a wine rated four stars (out
of five) in Platter's, with John Platter himself on hand as part of
the Gower tasting.

John Platter is a victim of collateral damage in the many and messy
fights involving the eponymous wine guide, which he sold a decade
ago. Which is perhaps to be expected as Platter is an old and venera-
ble brand. Historian Peter Ackroyd reports in *London* (Chatto & Win-
dus, 2001) that in the early 17th century, Thomas Platter described
'endless inns . . . beer and wine shops for every imaginable growth,
alicant, canary, muscatels, clarets, Spanish, Renish'. One wonders
whether the 'endless inns' paid to be included in that ancient Platter
guide, as is the case with the contemporary one.

Editors love it when inappropriate connoisseurs like Clarkson and
Gower pronounce on wine. But the big difference between Clarkson on cars and Platter on wine is that British motoring journalism
is consumer-driven, with Clarkson credited with single-handedly
destroying both the Vectra and the Vauxhall reputation, for example. Indeed, Clarkson's annual *Sunday Times* 'Car of the Year' feature highlights the worst as well as the best. By way of contrast, a
cynical summary of South African wine commentary as increasing
degrees of fabulousness would not be too far off the mark, paid for
as it often is by the wine producers themselves.

While indisputably useful, a list of the worst wines available to
consumers is unlikely, however, to gain much traction in the pro-
ducer-driven world of South African winespeak. With Clarkson's

main aim to entertain, his comments on cars, wines and life in general are hugely entertaining and a breath of fresh air – the kind you get driving a Jaguar XK with the hood down at 130mph.

Sometimes, the fickle finger of fate conspires to thrust connoisseurship into your lap.

ACCIDENTAL ONES

Sommeliers, or rather the lack of them, are one of the main differences between a South African fine-dining experience and the equivalent in France or Germany.

The approach run to the hamlet of Hattenheim, coming down from Kloster Eberbach, the medieval monastery where Umberto Eco's *The Name of the Rose* was filmed, was a bit of a challenge. An early March blizzard had dumped eight inches of snow onto the Rheingau. Here, in winter, if the snow tyres lose their grip on the cobbled street, either the suitably named ICE (Inter-City Express) or the medieval German masonry gets you. If you make the bend, you come to a half-timbered *Weinhaus* called Zum Krug. Most German restaurants seem to be called *zum* something or other and this one translates as 'zum jug'. Or *zum* very expensive French champagne.

Battling the blizzard from Frankfurt, we had stopped only once for a tasting at Weingut Künstler at Hochheim am Main. Of all the Rheingau Rieslings, like Rüdesheim, Johannisberg and Hochheim, Queen Victoria preferred the last, hence the generic term *Hoch* for a fine Rhine wine. Or, as Basil Fawlty might have put it, Vic certainly knew her Bordeaux from her claret.

The wines of Hochheim, and those of Gunter Künstler in particular, were assured of renewed British interest, with the winery displaying the FIFA logo on its Riesling labels in the run-up to the World Cup that summer. As the man pouring the wine in the *Weingut* put it, the aim was to offer an alternative to beer-swilling soccer hooligans (Riesling rioters, perhaps?). Quite how English

CONNOISSEURS

supporters pronounced names like Kirchenstück, Stielweg and Domdechaney was not reported.

There are differences between a Rheingau tasting and one in Rawsonville: the German affair was free and we were offered multiple vintages of two wines – a white (the inevitable Riesling) and a red, Spätburgunder (Pinot Noir to the rest of the world). At a Cape tasting, by contrast, every possible style is available, from sparkling to racy Sauvignon Blanc, woody Chardonnay, crackerjack Shiraz, a Boere-Bordeaux blend, rustic Pinotage, the odd sticky and perhaps a port.

Faced with an interminable crawl back to Frankfurt, a pit stop at 'zum jug' sounded like a good idea. Did it matter that we had no reservation, that unbeknown to us this was the second day of the Rheingau Gourmet and Wine Festival or even that we were wearing jeans from Mr Price? Not at all.

The youngest diners in the restaurant by a generation or two (and undoubtedly the poorest by an even larger margin), we were ushered into a wooden-clad inner sanctum complete with quasi-religious statues of St Vincent bearing a bunch of grapes by a band of waitress Valkyries. We were clearly in for some serious business if the heft of the wine list and the number of adjectives attached to each menu option was any indication.

With all the wines grown within spitting distance, the services of a good sommelier were not just nice to have, but essential. And this one certainly knew her Hock from her Riesling. She even had a favourable opinion of South African wine, having sampled an elegant Mont du Toit red blend on the island of Sylt in the North Sea. We started with a 2002 from Georg Breuer with a delicious concentration to match the home-cured *Lachs* and then moved on to something a touch sweeter from Winckelmann for the calf's liver.

The gift of a place like Zum Krug is making accidental connoisseurs out of refugees from a storm. In this age of pretentious gastronomic twaddle, with every *jus* now a foam and different shaped Riedels for sparkling and still water, this is the best kind of connoisseur to be.

GENUINE ONES

'But the bitch keeps bitching
snitcher keeps snitching
dropping names and telephone numbers and all . . . '

(M. JAGGER AND K. RICHARDS, *Little T&A*)

As I had already written a story for the *Sunday Times* throwing some
question marks at the inaugural Tasting Academy announced by
WINE magazine in 2007, which offered 'certificates of competency'
to successful punters, it would have been hypocritical of me to refuse
when invited to attend. Although the bill for R3,990 that followed
confirmed that this academy was no laughing matter.

The highlight turned out to be the UK wine identity imported first
class to give the affair some mega *gravitas*. Robert Parker described
Bristol wine merchant Bill Baker as 'a small and jealous person who
should consider selling refrigerators'. Rick Stein's popular BBC food
programme, 'Food Heroes', was bombarded with hate mail aimed at
Bill after he suggested Rick add some wheels and a motor to Chalky
when his beloved dog died.

Baker was a wine merchant from Bristol and consultant to Terence
Conran's international stable of restaurants one of the sharpest palates in the business. Bill put together the first wine list for Bibendum
and the Conran stable has grown like Topsy and now consists of 23
restaurants in London, three in Copenhagen and one in New York.

This Conran connection saves Bill from being regarded as a country hick wine merchant and he is shown (translation: gets to taste) all
the important imports into the UK, the largest market for imported
wine in the world.

A larger-than-life Falstaffian character with an infectious laugh,
Bill was star instructor at the Tasting Academy. Most of the time,
his opinion agreed with perceived South African wisdom, with the
embarrassing exception of a Chenin Blanc, awarded five stars by the

magazine two days before. Bill left it out of the medals, commenting, 'the acidity is all over the place. It won't keep'. But then his benchmark was the Loire. Which perhaps explains why Chenin is such a hard sell in Blighty, with different criteria clearly in play.

The Baker passion for food and wine was kindled at Peterhouse, Cambridge, while he was studying history of art:

> 'The dean of my college, a priest, had done someone a favour and had been given "a special bottle" of wine – which turned out to be a Château Latour '61. He invited a couple of us to taste it after dinner and I was blown away. I couldn't believe that something could be that powerful and that complex.'

A career as wine merchant at Reid Wines in the West Country followed, a fortunate choice, as UK wine consumption was on the brink of a hedonistic explosion, rather like that bottle of Latour thirty years ago. Explains Bill:

> 'There's been a huge change of lifestyle in the UK and dining out in restaurants has replaced drinking in pubs. Many pubs are turning into gastro-pubs and people are going out more and spending more money. There has been a huge rise in awareness around good food and wine.
>
> 'Twenty years ago the food was crap, but now you can find good food at every price level and the natural bev for food is wine. The rise and rise of rosé is a good example. Drinking rosé is seen as being sophisticated and the *Bridget Jones's Diary* thing had a huge effect on Chardonnay sales.'

While 85 per cent of the UK wine retail market is covered by supermarkets and bottle store chains, Bill notes that independent merchants offering something special are on the rise. Indeed, the only way to survive, he says, 'is to offer things the supermarkets don't have'.

Bill was surprised to hear that South African sales to the UK had fallen sharply, down 18 per cent on the previous year:

> 'Out in the countryside, people are very well disposed towards South Africa. In fact they'd much rather order a bottle of South African wine than French because they hate the French so much. At the entry level, prices of South African wines are slightly too high – the favourable rand/pound exchange rate often doesn't get translated into value in the bottle. You need the quality of Jacob's Creek at a similar price point to get people started buying South African on the quality ladder. But in the £5–£11 category, which we concentrate on, the quality of South African wine is extremely good and we have several South African wines on our list.'

Which includes examples from Thelema, Vergelegen, Warwick and Neil Ellis in the mid price range to the cult Columella Shiraz of Eben Sadie at £32.50 at the top. The list also contains a number of surprises:

> 'At the entry level we have some really good value Pinotage from Porterville – we usually buy either their Shiraz or Pinotage, depending on quality, and sometimes we buy both. Every restaurant wine list should include at least one South African Pinotage, but while there are some really good ones, there are also some shockers.

> 'Syrah is your most exciting varietal and I think it finds very good flavour expression here. The grapes have lovely spice and are better than many a Crozes Hermitage from France. Wine from Vergelegen and Sadie Family Vineyards are world class.'

On the subject of competition to South Africa in the all-important
UK market, Bill supplies some insights:

> 'Australia hasn't shot its bolt. They've had a couple of serious
> blows, with the current drought a major problem. They can't
> make wine as they've got no water, but don't write them off.
> The real excitement is going to come from South America.
> They're still struggling under a flood of bad wine but some
> excitement and value is starting to emerge.'

Americans – like Robert Parker and *Wine Spectator* magazine – have
totally messed up Bordeaux for Bill, 'although the French are starting to fight back'. In an attempt to garner high Parker scores, many
Bordeaux producers changed their style to more fruit expression
and higher alcohols. The popularity of these wines in the United
States pushed prices off the scale, 'a fate which is currently hap-
pening to top-end champagne and Madeira', laments Bill. 'But
wine is so global now, it's possible to find something interesting to
drink at all price points. The trick is to be satisfied with the level of
wine you can afford. It may not be Latour, but there are plenty of
second labels of French first growths around which can give huge
pleasure at the £14–£16 price point.'

Bill's bibulous future is more of the same: tasting and trading
'until I finish paying school fees for the children'. Then he'll sell
the business and retire to Italy, the unfashionable south appealing
to him. 'Tuscany is totally out of the question,' he booms, 'far too
many Brits.'

Alas, the future was to be tragically short. One week after returning from the 2008 Tasting Academy, Bill died in his sleep from a
massive heart attack.

Crisis? What crisis?

2007 was a year of crisis for South African wine. Or was it?

Urban legend has it that former British PM 'Sunny Jim' James Callaghan enquired 'Crisis? What crisis?' upon arriving back in the UK after a summit in sunny Guadeloupe in the middle of Britain's Winter of Discontent – a period when even the gravediggers were out on strike. The truth is that it was actually an unknown subeditor at *The Sun* whose three-word headline summed up how out of touch the British government was with the state of affairs in its borders.

First reports of a crisis in South African wine also originated in the British press. In March 2007, *Decanter* magazine reported: 'South African winegrowers are being forced out of business as prices drop due to oversupply . . . as well as falling exports, slow domestic sales, unstable exchange rates and farm subsidies in rival wine-producing countries.'

But then, wasn't it always so? It was Jan Smuts who pointed out that the only thing a farmer can grow without a subsidy is a moustache.

The big boys of South African wine certainly weren't ringing any alarm bells. Ernst le Roux, group manager for grape and wine production at Distell, South Africa's largest wine producer, said in reaction to the *Decanter* story:

> 'I've seen the newspaper reports of . . . wine farms for sale in Stellenbosch, but I monitor farm sales and have not seen a single one this year, so things can't be that bad if asking prices are still too high.

> 'It's also wrong to think that Stellenbosch represents the whole industry. It accounts for 12 per cent of the total crop and while farmers in low production areas, like the coastal

region, are definitely hurting from lower prices for grapes, farmers on the Orange River, who harvest 35 tonnes of grapes per hectare and get R1,500 per tonne for them, are still making good money. And the industry is not only wine. We're making good money from brandy.'

Le Roux insisted rumours of the death of South African wine had been greatly exaggerated:

'With farm prices so high, we're still not in a crisis. Futurologist Professor Spies used to say the problem is that farmers are price-driven and not market-driven. When there was a red wine shortage, prices were high and so farmers planted red grapes. Now there is a surplus and prices have fallen.

'It's the capitalist system. The economics of grape farming has changed: we're moving out of a system of protection and surplus removal into more of a free-market system. Not everyone will make it and some producers will go under. Of the prices I've seen asked for farms, they are still not production related. A few farms were sold for silly money last year and now everyone is looking for a price way above economic value.'

Like Klein Vondeling in the recently proclaimed Voor Paardeberg appellation between Paarl and Durbanville. On the market for R7.5 million, when the owner was offered his asking price by Albert Roux (whose Le Gavroche in London was Britain's first Michelin three-star restaurant), it was hastily withdrawn from the market. The owner'srationale being 'if you accept my offer price, I've obviously underpriced the property'. Thereby denying South Africa its best shot at a Michelin star.

Albert's revenge – to trash the author's favourite steakhouse, Belthazar, on Cape Town's Waterfront – was not long in coming.

Details of a liquid lunch at Belthazar, were soon leaked to the South African press. The lunch started with a bottle of Warwick Trilogy for R1,200. So far, so touristique.

That being the last bottle in stock and Albert being thirsty, a similar wine was offered by what turned out to be 'a naïve and overzealous manager', who charged the party R7,000 for a 1982 Meerlust Cabernet.

What was missing from the story is that it was a magnum and Meerlust 82 is very much a trophy wine – the South African equivalent of a Bordeaux first growth (from a good year). Albert's comment on the price of the bottle was: 'This country has a lot to learn.' Instead, it should have been punted as the deal that it was. After all, £450 in Albert's own establishment would be something of a steal for such a wine.

Perhaps a more real crisis in South African wine is a crisis of faith. Not so much a lack, but confusion, of allegiance between two powerful gods: Bacchus and Mammon. This was brought into focus by the launch of two red blends at the end of 2007: Waterford's The Jem 2004 at R680 a bottle and the Quintette 2005 from Spar at around 10 per cent of that. Both have impeccable credentials. The former was made by Kevin Arnold, a leading light in the Cape Winemakers' Guild and the man who put Rust en Vrede on the quality map. The latter was blended by Tinus van Niekerk. Owner of one of the sharpest palates in the business, Van Niekerk makes Formula One wines in terroirs as diverse as the Orange River, Robertson and the Rhône.

Both cuvées hail from Stellenbosch, with fruit for The Jem from the Helderberg, while the five components of the latter come from Spier. Similarities aside, they are poles apart in one important department: price. Why?

Perhaps the first lesson they should teach at the UCT Business School course on wine marketing is that fine wine has nothing to do with economics. Fine wine is becoming increasingly like perfume and haute couture: it is aspiration that is being sold, rather

than the contents of the bottle. When winemakers slip through the
grape curtain to showcase their products at winemaker dinners, the
venues are invariably the swankiest restaurants.

Sybrand van der Spuy owns Cape Point Vineyards, currently the
Cape's most successful winery as measured by wine show geegaws
and yet another award in Platter's. Sybrand will tell you with a dis-
arming smile that he only loses R40 on each bottle of wine he sells.
Such is the cost of opening up a whole new appellation – in his case
planting vineyards at Scarborough and Fish Hoek. Fellow financial mogul, Dave King, and other wine-loving pioneers at Agulhas
would probably say that Sybrand got a good deal at a loss of only
R40 per bottle.

Priced at the leading edge of aspiration, served in expensive crystal stemware with outsize bowls and with auction prices becoming
more and more rarified, fine wine frequently hops from the pages of
the lifestyle supplement onto the front page of the *Financial Times*.
Forbes falls over itself to validate conspicuous consumption as fine
wine moves onto the heady heights populated by fine art.

It's a no-brainer for producer and punter. High prices are an
excellent abbreviation for concepts that the moneyed punter doesn't
necessarily understand. It's a cruel twist of fate that most of the
palates buying these highly priced Bacchanalian reliquaries are on
the angel's side of fifty, with palates past their physiological prime
and egos just about the only facility left with which to appreciate
expensive goodies.

So what does it all mean, apart from a fat pay day for a few lucky
producers and the usual insiders? In focusing on high price, South
African wine runs the risk of falling into a trap.

Take WOSA's reaction to the news that Chile is expected to over-
take South Africa as fifth largest supplier to the all-important UK
wine market sooner rather than later. *Harpers* reported it as follows:

> 'Jo Mason, UK market manager for Wines of South Afri-
> ca, said she was not disappointed that Chile had overtaken

South Africa in the multiples. Despite a fall in sales of 5 per cent by volume and value this year, she pointed out that its average price had increased in the same period and was higher than Chile's (£3.80).'

Chile's average price is given as £3.72, but its volumes are up 26 per cent and value by 23 per cent on the year, so you don't need to hire Raymond Ackerman as a consultant to discover whose business is in better shape.

In the wake of South Africa's disastrous performance in the controversial 1995 South African Airways wine test match between South Africa and Australia, the organisers turned their sights to a triangular tourney, with Down Under replaced by a Chile and Argentina double act. After South African industry backlash to the Aussie defeat, the new series was abandoned before it grew legs. But at least a couple of South African wine hacks – including yours truly – had an enjoyable meal in a fabulous restaurant on the shores of Lake Garda in the company of Douglas Murray, founder of Montes, a serious Chilean wine producer.

A decade ago, South Africa would almost certainly have triumphed, especially if the judges were specially chosen (a situation, some would argue, that explained the poor showing of South Africa against the kangaroos).

But ten years is a long time in wine and after six weeks spent sipping Chilean Carmenère and Cabernet in Belo Horizonte at spectacularly good value for money, with juicy Argentinian Malbec on the side, this punter would now back the South American gods of value who are in the ascendant over Mammon, so fervently worshipped in the South African cellar.

Back in the vineyard, while farmers may not yet be *inspanning* the oxen and preparing to trek north again, exports are on a roller coaster. Shipments to the UK slumped from 102 million litres in 2005 to 87 million in 2006, with some recovery in 2007. (WOSA supply a semi-plausible explanation for the 2005/6 slump: brand leader Kumala was sold to some Canadians who sold it to some Americans . . . who lost the plot.)

This confirms the opinion of Robert Joseph, chairman of judges at the 2007 Swiss International Air Lines Wine Awards, whose contention was: 'The top South African brands in the UK, like Kumala and Golden Kaan, are owned and produced by foreigners, which is not a healthy situation to be in. With Kumala sales down 800,000 cases, leaving your export market in foreign hands is a dodgy strategy for South African wine.'

But there could be a more prosaic explanation. Seems the export slide is all the fault of our tongue-twisting South African names, like Vergelegen, Buitenverwachting, Fleermuisklip and Agterkliphoogte, which play pyrotechnics with the tonsils.

While brash Americans are happy to order a bottle of 'bite me for watching' (Buitenverwachting), Brits are more skittish and prefer to order something they can pronounce. In fact, a survey of 200 young London professionals conducted by the Devon-based Ashburton Cookery School, reported in *The Guardian*, revealed that three-quarters of respondents 'will not order dishes or drinks if they think there is a risk that they might mispronounce the name'.

Some other gems include the admission that 'during business lunches, 65 per cent of young professionals questioned have made food or wine choices based upon their desire to impress others rather than what they actually want'. And if their choices fail to live up to expectation, '63 per cent of respondents say they would rather sit in silence than cause a scene by sending back unsatisfactory food'. So far, so Johannesburg northern suburbs.

This habit, however, of only ordering wines you can pronounce is not restricted to yuppie diners. Wine buyers for Virgin Wines in the UK obviously employ the same algorithm if their South African selection is anything to go by: Three Gables, Churchaven, Radford Dale, Good Hope, The Plume and Brahms. Most of them are unknown even to Platter's, but at least pronounceable and sound like they were made in the Home Counties.

Their only tricky brand from a pronunciation point of view is Kaapzicht, but then Danie Steytler can always fall back on his Cape View range – specially introduced for the Dutch who thought that Kaapzicht, the historical name of the farm, was a transparent attempt to curry favour with Dutch consumers by using a Dutch name.

Buitenverwachting owner Lars Maack pointed out that the name issue is one of authenticity versus marketability when he was asked by his US distributor to change the brand name for Buitenverwachting Buiten Blanc. Which he duly did, adopting the clever compromise of 'Beyond', a partial translation of Buitenverwachting, which is retained as the producer on the back label. This might suggest a neat, pronounceable replacement for Nabygelegen as 'Near' and Vergelegen as 'Far' (although Napa producer Far Niente might not be too happy with this).

SONOROUS SIPPING

Faced with thousands of wine brands, vocalising their names and choosing the most musical is not a bad strategy.

As an aside, it's worth noting that wine is not the only commodity bought by ear. French writer Marcel Proust would dabble on the Paris stock exchange, selecting shares according to a novel algorithm – the sound of their names. This explains his mellifluous portfolio: Pins des Landes, Malacca Rubber Plantations and his favourite: S. A. Chemin de Fer de Rosario à Puerto Belgrano.

Proust applied a similar algorithm to his friends, with 'their alluring beauty' being the sonority of their titles. Richard Davenport-Hines notes in his fascinating memoir of the great modernist dinner party of 1922, *A Night at the Majestic*, that Gladys, the Duchess of Marlborough, recalled the novelist 'succulently' murmuring resonant titles to himself.

When it comes to French wines, aurally, Domaine de la Romanée-Conti is the grandest of grand Burgundies, while Château Pichon Longueville Comtesse de Lalande rings the sexiest of the super second growths of Bordeaux. Pichon used to be owned by Madame May-Eliane de Lencquesaing, who recently sold a controlling interest to Louis Roederer, makers of that mega-bling brand Cristal champagne, popular with American rappers and their fans.

Octogenarian May is now focusing her attention on making wine in Stellenbosch with the altogether less sonorous moniker of Glenelly Hills, which sounds more like a whisky or a golf course. While she waits for a cellar to be built, her vintages are made at Quoin Rock – another low scorer in the pronunciation stakes, but at least appropriately named, as Quoin Rock is a neighbouring cellar owned by financial outsourcing mogul and art collector Dave King.

When the *Financial Mail* reported that May and Dave were discussing a joint venture back in 2004, feisty May fired off a fragrant letter to the editor, stating that she had been introduced to King by *Business Day* wine pundit Michael Fridjhon, who suggested a joint venture brand.

May declined after 'having become aware of reports published in the South African press regarding King'. So it was nice to see that, three years later, Dave has been rehabilitated because he really is an excellent chap to have to dinner, as he often brings bottles of icon wine from the cellar he bought from Jurgen Harksen. I thoroughly enjoyed the Haut Brion '66 and it was a real pity he dropped the magnum of May's '38 Pichon Lalande. The penny only dropped much later that his companion, Kenny Dalgleish, was a soccer hero of note. I just thought he looked athletic.

Like Dave, May has been warmly welcomed by her neighbours and the industry in general. Unable to pronounce De Lencquesaing, farm workers on neighbouring Rustenberg estate refer to her as 'madam hier langsaan' (madam next door) – which rhymes with her name.

Invited to open the annual Nederburg Auction in 2004, I had the pleasure of sitting next to her at the post-auction dinner held at the Grande Roche (Big Cockroach, to the winepress), a German-owned hotel in the Winelands of Paarl. She was in fine form, with stories of her travelling companion, a pet monkey usually to be found sitting on her shoulder. A touch of the exotic, perhaps inherited from a Philippine grandmother, further up her family tree.

Some of her secrets are revealed in Don and Petie Kladstrup's *Wine and War*, (Broadway, 2002) like how her family hid Jewish refugees from the Nazis during the Second World War. When I suggested she write her autobiography, however (a no-brainer bestseller), she cried off, saying she was much too busy. When I offered to ghost it, she said: 'But I don't know you.'

'Even better,' I replied. But she wouldn't be persuaded and her lips went all skinny.

On the subject of ghosts, she related how of an evening she would recount events of the day to the portraits of her ancestors which hung in the chateau.

'And did they ever reply?'

'Sometimes,' she said with a twinkle in her eye.

AS SMOOTH AS SLATE

Mr Harksen and his cellar popped up again in 2008.

Constantia's vineyards are rapidly becoming the monoculture of the suburb, taking the process started by Jan van Riebeeck and Simon van der Stel to its logical conclusion of replacing all indigenous fynbos with that commercially valuable invader, *Vitis vinifera*.

Calling your *pied à Constantia* Falcon's Eye is appropriate on many levels. The burgeoning vineyards of Constantia are full of eagle eyes – glass pyramids that refract light and so act as mini-scarecrows to the flocks of *mossies* and jackal buzzards that would feast on the ripening grapes. Manxman Jonathan Mylrea, further up Constantiaberg in his eyrie called Eagle's Nest, prefers CDs suspended on fishing gut (classical tunes only) to achieve the same effect.

The banks of spy cameras and electronic eyes, which swivel and watch as you stroll up Belair Drive above Groot Constantia, protect the assets and secrets of perhaps the densest concentration of wealth on the continent.

And then there are clear parallels to Goldeneye, the 17th Bond film: Constantia was once, in the naughty nineties, the lair of German financial fraudster Jurgen Harksen. As the *EP Herald* hilariously described him, 'Going bald in his 20s, the moon-faced Harksen hardly resembled the good-looking Leonardo DiCaprio, conman character in the movie *Catch Me if You Can*. Harksen managed to scam the high society of Hamburg – said to have more millionaires than any other city in Germany – with Ponzi schemes and pyramid investments galore.

Hamburg also happens to be the home town of the current inhabitant of Falcon's Eye, Christian Gebranzig, who has substantial investments in the hospitality industry and a wine distribution company based in the city. This bacchanalian passion he evidently shares with Harksen, whose cellar was touted around Johannesburg for a rumoured R1 million until snapped up by billionaire Dave King at a healthy discount, according to urban legend.

The connection to Goldeneye is apposite: Falcon's Eye looks like something out of a James Bond film. Stainless steel front door from a U-boat (or a bank vault); pergola with Indiana Jones wooden suspension bridge inspired by Sol Kerzner's Sun City and the outsize furniture for giants beloved of interior designers in bright nursery colours. A most appropriate venue for a Germanic wine tasting (with the exception of climate control, sorely missed on a Sunday with unseasonal Durbanesque humidity).

Put together by Aubergine sommelier Jörg Pfützner, the tasting featured the Kaiser of German Riesling, Ernie Loosen, from iconic producer Dr Loosen, and the brittle wines of Dirk van der Niepoort, whose mom also hails from the Fatherland.

Billed as a Slate Tasting, the brief was to showcase wines grown on slate, the metamorphic rock derived from shale through the application of millions of years and billions of bars of pressure. In South Africa, wines grown on shale, like those of Willie de Waal at Scali (the Afrikaans for shale is 'skalie') on the Paardeberg, are currently all the rage, exhibiting a fine-boned minerality that raises the flavours from a boring fruity profile to complexity city, with whiffs of flint and studied concentration.

Eben Sadie, who lives on Scali, is the foremost proponent of this style of wine in South Africa. He has some serious success under his vest – his Columella blend of Shiraz and Mourvèdre is the first South African wine to rate a classic (95/100) score in US magazine *Wine Spectator* (even if it was not considered worthy enough to make the five-star tasting in the 2008 *Platter's*).

And just like the five-star accolade, Sadie and his Shiraz were conspicuous by their absence from Falcon's Eye. Three explanations were doing the rounds: hangover from the previous night's tasting at Aubergine; involvement with the 2008 harvest already underway, and unseasonal rain. My money is on a combination of all three. Or perhaps he was running late, as his Swartland wines grow on shale that takes around 270 million years to transform into slate. In the meantime, he'll have to make do with those he grows in Priorat, Spain, on *llicorella* – brown slate.

With hindsight, the Sadie no-show was just as well – after six hours of tasting and eating (Aubergine chef Harald Bresselschmidt wore the toque), Niepoort had only reached his middle-order reds. I'd prepared for the tasting by reading Truman Capote's essay on Santorini.

Moored off the Mediterranean island in 1968 on a yacht similar to Harksen's *Wall Street*, the guest of some billionaire playboy or other, Capote records he was not a big fan of Greek wine, with the exception of King Minos – a spicy white made without the addition of pine resin, which was the status quo for Greek wines back then. The prospect of walking up thousands of steps to the top of the mountain had made him opt for a bottle of local vino and two peaches the size of cantaloupes. The great society scribbler marvelled at how such barren soil (a mixture of slate, chalk, coal, ash, lava and pumice) could produce such intense flavours.

Ernie Loosen was only slightly less poetic when describing the range of Rieslings his family has been growing on precipitous slopes above the Mosel River for the past two centuries, but made essentially the same point. Slate confers immunity to phylloxera, the louse inadvertently imported from America in the nineteenth century and which laid waste to the vineyards of the Old World. Loosen's Riesling vines still grow on their original rootstock, while the competition in Alsace and elsewhere have to be grafted onto American rootstocks, immune to the louse. Another factor is the high potassium content of slate soils, which increases acid levels in the grapes, and low vigour means good concentration of flavours in the berries.

Niepoort was more cerebral and his wines more of a challenge. His 2006 whites are incredibly acidic and will require many years in bottle – commercial suicide in these impatient days of immediate consumption: bottles bought in the supermarket are typically drunk the same day. But then it was a bottle of 1938 *vinho consumo* (Portuguese *vin ordinaire*) from an antique shop that opened his eyes to the ageing potential of wines from Portugal and the Douro in particular.

Reds are Niepoort's strong suit, but his dismissal of 'a Coca-Cola world in which everything is sweeter' is a challenge, as is his denial of the primacy of fruit. 'I don't like a lot of fruit. I want zingy acidity and freshness. I don't believe in varietals,' he continues, provocatively. Giving cultivars the flick is a potent rejection of New World-style winemaking, with brands sorted by cultivar on the supermarket shelf and blends unscrambled into constituent cultivars on the back label:

'Don't ask me the grapes in this blend – I don't know. There could be two dozen varietals. My objective is to have as much natural acid as possible. We harvest them all at the same time. Strangely, they all ripen together, which is not the case when they grow in separate vineyards. We wait until they're mostly ripe, at the stage when around 10 per cent are underripe and 10 per cent are overripe.'

His observation of synchronised ripening is probably due to pheromones, plant hormones, which in the human context are an explanation for the synchronisation of the menstrual cycles of girls in a boarding school. The archetypal angry young man, Niepoort is shaking things up in the Douro, an appellation more famous for its ports than elegant reds. As is his patronymic, which he shares with one of the great port brands owned by his family. That he is now making table wine rather than Port is like the son of Ronald McDonald joining Slow Food.

His wines make a statement, as does the man himself. Niepoort on Portuguese viniculture: 'Two thousand years of making bad wines.' On the flagship Portuguese varietal, Touriga Naçional: 'The disaster of Portugal. It is a grape with a lot of character and everyone's planting it. Soon everything will taste the same.'

A situation that will not happen in South Africa if Pfützner and his Slate Tastings become a fixture on the local wine calendar. These wines pose a forceful challenge to that dangerous feeling of contentment that comes from drinking only South African wine and ends in mediocrity. By presenting winemakers who contend that a serious red blend can be made without wood maturation (Niepoort), or who have a violent reaction to high alcohol levels (Loosen), Pfützner is performing a valuable service for the South African wine-drinking public. Just the kind of thing you'd expect from an über-sommelier.

RUNNING OFF TO JOIN THE CIRCUS

*Some observations on the epidemic of competitions that has seized
South African wine by the pocket.*

'The fat lady of Limbourg
looked at the samples that we sent
and furrowed her brow.
You would never believe that
she'd tasted royalty and fame
if you saw her now.
But her sense of taste is such that she'll distinguish with her
tongue
the subtleties a spectrograph would miss,
and announce her decision,
while demanding her reward:
the jellyfish kiss.'

(BRIAN ENO, *The Fat Lady of Limbourg*)

The question of hedonistic choice is a serious one. It was addressed
by the beauty columnist of the *Financial Times Weekend*, Edwina
Ings-Chambers, who asked the ultimate Miss World question: 'How
should beauty be judged?'

This was no Platonic discussion for its own sake, but a meditation
on why Pond's Cold Cream failed to make the finals of the Cos-
metic Executive Women Beauty Awards, where such exotic slap as
Clarins Super Restorative Redefining Body Care and Elemis Tri-
Enzyme Resurfacing Serum tied for first place.

As Ings-Chambers noted, 'We all think we know what beauty is;
we apply – theoretically at least – a set of easy-to-follow formulae.'
In the case of wine, the judging process usually involves a quali-
tative assessment of faults followed by a process of ticking style
boxes. At one of the wine shows popular with South African pro-

ducers, the Concours Mondial de Bruxelles (held, confusingly, in Lisbon in 2006, Maastricht in 2007 and Bordeaux in 2008), these boxes are gnomically labelled 'limpidity' and 'genuineness'.

Quite how you rate genuineness in a wine tasted blind is a moot point. If it is a tart Portuguese Vinho Verde you can't mark it down for excessive acidity as that's the wine's style. Picking up oxidative character on a Madeira is likewise a plus but a no-no for other whites. Genuineness is indeed hard to score when the only ancillary information you have is vintage.

Australia's head honcho when it comes to tasting, James Halliday, admitted: you decide if the wine is worth a medal and then reverse engineer the box-ticking process to ensure the result. Something La Motte winemaker Edmund Terblanche got down to a fine art, with no fewer than five of his wines winning gold at the 2007 tourney.

Shiraz was the most popular South African varietal, with more than one-third of South African golds made from this sexy cultivar and the only South African Grand Gold (Fairview Solitude Shiraz 2004). It was the same story at the Swiss International Airlines Wine Awards, with Shiraz golds for Asara, Lynx, Rietvallei, Saronsberg (two) and Stellenzicht, while the *Wine Spectator* called the cultivar: 'South Africa's top varietal . . . combining a New World fruit profile with Old World elegance' in an article entitled 'South Africa's Serious Syrahs', published in March 2007.

In the fourth revised edition of a spectacularly error-prone *Sotheby's Wine Encyclopedia* (Dorling Kindersley, 2007), Tom Stevenson notes that South African Shiraz 'can give most Australian Shiraz a run for their money. This must now be regarded as South Africa's most exciting red variety.' (Or was this comment yet another of Tom's schoolboy howlers, with South African Shiraz really 'rubbish', Jeremy Clarkson's immortal opinion?)

The latter seemed to be the conclusion reached by Ings-Chambers' FT colleague, UK first lady of wine Jancis Robinson MW OBE, after a day sipping the stuff at the annual Old Mutual

Trophy Wine Show – or Toasty Show as it is fondly known – a competition owned by Michael Fridjhon.

The adviser to the cellars of Her Majesty QEII (as the press
release vouchsafed in a crescendo of cultural cringe) together
with respected Meerlust winemaker Chris Williams and Gary
Jordan of Jordan Wines could find only a single gold medal-
ist in the shape of Dave King's Quoin Rock from a flight of
151 young Shiraz and Syrahs. Thus confirming that Fridjhon's
proposed Bordeaux partner for Madame May also has serious
Rhônish credentials.

Not that cellar adviser to a royal is a job to be taken lightly. Perhaps the most famous was Galen, personal physician to Roman
Emperor Marcus Aurelius. Galen's job was to find the best wine
in the world so his boss could wash down *theriac*, a universal antidote to poison and general pick-me-up that Galen prescribed.
Based on a secret recipe of Mithradates, king of Pontus, it was
made from ground-up lizard, poppy juice, spices, incense, juniper
berries, ginger, hemlock seed, raisins, fennel, aniseed and licorice,
according to Tom Standage in *A History of the World in Six Glasses*
(Atlantic, 2005).

And of course, Galen's task was much easier than a Toasty Show
tasting – there were only 80 wines of note in ancient Roman times
and two-thirds of those were grown in what would later be known as
Italy. Falernian, from the slopes of Mount Falernus, south of Naples,
was the undisputed first growth. So Galen started with it:

> '[I] submitted to my palate every wine over 20 years old. I
> kept on until I found a wine without a trace of bitterness.'

Marcus Aurelius died in 180 CE after a week of *theriac* and Falernian and with him, the golden age of the Roman Empire.

Back at the Toasty Show – the nickname refers to a sadly defunct
e.TV breakfast show with a cast of bizarre characters strangely reminiscent of wine show judges and Roman Emperors – the whites

fared better than the reds. There were two white golds for every red and, in a low blow to traditionalists, a wine closed by a screw cap was voted best white of show – a Chardonnay from Backsberg, where the ubiquitous Fridjhon also serves as chairman.

This is a common occurrence in the dizzy world of wine shows. Tony Bish, chairman of judges at the Hawkes Bay Wine Awards and owner of Gunn Estate, was faced with the same problem later in 2007. Except Bish did the noble thing and withdrew his Skeetfield Chardonnay 2006 from the competition to avoid presenting the Champion Wine Trophy to himself.

Indeed, inconsistency and conflicts of interest give South African wine competitions a credibility chasm like the ones opening up in the Greenland ice sheet through global warming. A 2006 scandal in the New Zealand wine spittoon was the inconvenient truth (*pace* Al Gore) that wines submitted to competitions are not necessarily the same as the ones on the supermarket shelf.

Close on the heels of conflicts of interest, one of the most telling arguments against choosing wine by show results is the logistics of the process. The task set the Toasty judges is a demanding one indeed, with more wines rated in a single day than a Concours judge would dare tackle over three. Springfield winemaker Abrie Bruwer memorably told me:

> 'If you think I'm going to pay you R1,000 to sniff and sip my wine for 30 seconds and then pass an opinion on something that's taken me a year and a lifetime to produce, you must be crazy.'

Just how desperate some producers are to shift product is reflected in the many hundreds of entries the numerous local wine competitions attract. Given that there are now over two dozen South African wine competitions, the show circus consumes sizeable resources from producers. And if you take into account the overseas beauty contests, like the International Wine Challenge, International Wine and Spirit Competition, *Decanter* World Wine Awards and a host of specialist single varietal tourneys, wine shows comprise a significant proportion of production and marketing costs.

One medium-sized Sellenbosch producer reckons that stickers for Veritas, the largest South African wine show, cost 80c each – 2c for the sticker and 78c for competition entry costs, tasting samples, promotional bottles and administrative overhead. A sizeable amount for a wine that retails at R40 a bottle, as this particular one does. In the case of Veritas, an entry is almost guaranteed a medal so in practice, 80c is the cost of a sticker. For other shows, however, the chances of recognition are far smaller, in effect increasing sticker costs by a factor proportional to the odds of getting one.

Nonetheless, producers obviously think the game is worth the candle, as entries (unlike sales) remain buoyant and each year record numbers of entries are recorded. A survey of producers by winemaker and *GQ* columnist Alex Dale produced the not-too-surprising result that show organisers were perceived as the main beneficiaries of shows, with consumers placed last.

The conclusion is confirmed by a letter to the editor of *WINE* that was selected for the coveted prize of a magnum of Dom Pérignon for best submission. Reflecting on 2005, the reader noted:

> 'One thing the year finally taught me was to regard wine competitions as mere opinions and not as wine gospel. My biggest disappointment was how unconvincing the winners of the Trophy Wine Show were. No one will convince me that the winning blends of Cabernet and Merlot are truly our best wines. In my (mere) opinion, they are undrinkable, heavy-footed and so tannin-laden that I wanted to give my mouth mouth-to-water resuscitation!'

Picking such a critical letter as winning correspondence indicates either sabotage or a welcome ability to laugh at yourself (*WINE* supplies logistics for the Toasty Show). Either way, the message is bad news indeed for the competition circus. *WINE* readers are presumably the punters who would seek out show winners, especially those with enough energy to write letters to the ed. A widespread loss of confidence in show results would surely bring down the curtain at the circus.

My own Road to Damascus moment, when I realised the limitations of shows, also happened at the Toasty Show. I was a judge for the first four years of its existence, until retired to let others have a turn. (At least that's what I was told at the time. Later on, it emerged that I was fired.) France's most eminent commentator, Michel Bettane, was asked to chair the Sauvignon Blanc panel. 'Of course not,' was his response. 'I know nothing about South African Sauvignon.' The man used to be a professor of philosophy at Fontainebleau.

Next in status, the job fell to me. After evaluating a couple of wines for calibration, I asked Michel for his scores. '60 and 80,' was the reply. '80 if you like this style of wine. 60 if you don't.' So either a silver medal, or nothing.

But if not shows, then what? The last time I was in Manhattan, I nearly stood on Woody Allen. If it hadn't been for Soon-Yi at his side, I would have. Seriously shaken, I decided to have lunch at Onera, a Greek restaurant on the Upper West Side. The owner, a Sydneysider of Greek origin, recommended a Xinomavro to accompany the meze platter. As full bodied, tannic and bold as a woody Pinotage, it sold me on modern Greek reds – without a single show medal on the bottle.

Sometimes I really wish Pieter de Waal would carry out his threat to add his own medal to his Hermit on the Hill Shiraz – a gold roundel with the words 'this wine has not been entered into any wine show' decorating the border.

THE TALE OF A NOSE

The most bizarre tsunami in the South African wine spittoon occurred in
2007 when a short story by Nikolai Gogol played out in the Winelands.
The profession of food taster is a noble one, with several giving
their lives to protect their employers. Screenwriter Peter Elbling
had a best-seller on his hands with *The Food Taster*, a surreal faux-
memoir of a 16th-century Italian food taster, Ugo DiFonte, defending his employer, the corrupt Duke Federico Basillione DiVincelli,
against such poisons as the saliva of a pig hung upside down and
beaten until it went mad.

Fidel Castro had one and Alexander Litvinenko, who died of
polonium poisoning, could have done with one. The Borgias used
them extensively, as did the Russian royals.

Which sets the scene for Gogol's surreal story of Collegiate Assessor
Kovalyov, who wakes one morning to discover his nose missing.

Kovalyov's nose turns up in the breakfast roll of his barber, who
tosses it into St Petersburg's River Neva. The nose decides to pur-
sue an independent career and finds employment as a state coun-
cillor with elegant carriage and a smart uniform. A bit like the cosy
club of international wine judges in their Blundstones and Issey
Miyakes in business class, which has superseded the elegant car-
riages of yore.

Gogol's surreal story could be behind the reason Robert Parker
has insured his own proboscis for $1 million. For without it, Park-
er would be like Kovalyov, who battled to have his opinions taken
seriously *sans nez*. It may have been one of the motivations behind
Dutch winemaker and musician Ilya Gort insuring his nose for R60
million in 2008 with Lloyd's of London.

Gort is the owner of Château de la Garde in Bordeaux, and his
wine was voted best Bordeaux of 2003 at the International Wine
Challenge in London. He is also a published author: *Het Wijnsur-*
vivalboek is one of his.

While insuring your sharp end might be easily dismissed as PR grandstanding along the lines of Betty Grable insuring her legs for $1 million apiece or Dolly Parton her 106 cm embonpoint for $600,000, losing your sense of smell does happen.

Ask Bernd Philippi, who was voted Germany's top winemaker in *Feinschmecker* magazine for his iconic Saumagen (sow's stomach) Riesling. Philippi lost his sense of smell when he banged the back of his head during a fall. A whizz at blending and responsible for the 2001 Mont du Toit, which *Decanter* hailed as the best South African Bordeaux blend (embarrassing Shiraz component notwithstanding) and which impressed the *zum jug* sommelier so (see p20, *Connoisseurs – Accidental ones*), Philippi now relies on flavour and the tactile impression of viscosity, although his nasal acuity is slowly returning.

Of course, many are fervently hoping that Parker's insurers will have to cough up. Philosopher Roger Scruton, who writes the most erudite wine column in the business for the *New Statesman*, noted:

> 'Thanks to Nosy Parker, the entire market in wine has been surrendered to the phony expertise of the modern oenophile, which consists in writing execrable prose about flavours, awarding arbitrary points and pretending to be a nose about town.'

Scruton's main gripe is that the application of Parker's proboscis reduces centuries of French tradition, mystique and terroir to a common denominator that may be compared with the brash New World. No bad thing, some would say. My own problem is not with Parker's schnozzle per se (and judging by photographs, it's an outwardly inoffensive organ), just the fact that his is the only nose in town.

With John Platter now moved on to better things, like rounds of golf in KwaZulu-Natal, South Africa has no serious contender for a R1 million 'nose about town'. Imports are quoted along with their Parker ratings and local recommendations are usually the result of committee decisions of wine shows and magazine tasting panels. Platter's personal proboscis has been replaced by a panel of 'professional' hooters. Around two dozen in number, they come in all shapes and sizes, with the handful of annual wine guides featuring the opinions of a subset across multiple publications. While not as extreme as the Parker mono-nose model, the lack of nasal diversity is an issue.

Reflecting on the 'Dark Side of Wine' in his *Wine Buyer's Guide*, Parker highlights 'the growing international standardisation of wine styles' as issue number one. A standardisation, ironically, he has done most to advance through his overwhelming dominance in the business of compiling liquid laundry lists.

If you accept that variety, as well as being the spice of life, is one of the features that makes wine more exciting than premixed cocktails and ready-to-drinks, where are the new noses for sniffing out icons to come from? Perhaps the burgeoning restaurant scene in a shopping centre near you holds the key. With more wine dinners and chefs' tables than you can shake a swizzle stick at, perhaps the time has come for the opinions of sommeliers, maître d's and chefs to achieve wider currency. They certainly can't do any worse than the present lot.

The public is heartily sick and tired of show-off noses, if the theft of a statue to Gogol's nose in St Petersburg is anything to go by. The 100 kg marble schnozzle 'seems to have gone for a walk', according to its sculptor, Vyacheslav Bukhayev. 'I really don't know who could have taken it – maybe it was some art lover who prefers admiring works of art in private.'

Artthrob reports that the darling of the corporate art collection, William Kentridge, after a smash hit with Mozart's *Magic Flute* in 2007, is now working towards a 2010 production of Shostakovich's opera *The Nose* at the Met in New York. If six winemakers were prepared to shell out R50,000 each for the rights to use a flute image as a label, how much more might they pay to embrace Shostakovitch's nose?

But the R50,000 question ignored by Gogol and Shostakovich is: what did Kovalyov do in the interim before he was reunited with his shnoz? Moonlight as a wine judge? At the 2007 outing of the Toasty Show, a British Master of Wine of mega gravitas rated more than a gross of Shiraz 'with no sense of smell whatever' and there's been a funny smell in the air ever since. 'My sore throat turned into one of the worst fluey colds I can remember,' this latter-day Kovalyov confided to the subscription-only pages of her website.

Instead of retiring injured, claiming against the insurance policy, or at least keeping mum, she valiantly pressed on and did it all by mouth. 'It has been really interesting to have my senses focussed [*sic*] on the structure of each wine and on what you can sense only with the palate,' she remarked, which must have caused much wailing and gnashing of teeth among the Pinelands pundits at *WINE* magazine, who had to print her comments on South African wine with a straight face. Producers were not best pleased.

The comments of La Kovalyov fly in the face of perceived wisdom. The first philosopher of taste since Epicurus, the renowned French gastronome Jean Anthelme Brillat-Savarin, authoritatively recognised the importance of smell back in 1825 in his landmark *Physiology of Taste*:

> 'I am not only convinced that without the cooperation of smell there can be no complete degustation,' he noted, 'but I am also tempted to believe that smell and taste are in fact but a single sense, whose laboratory is in the mouth and whose chimney is the nose; or to be more precise, in which the mouth performs the degustation of the tactile bodies, and the nose the degustation of the gases.'

It is self-evident that food and drink lose their flavour and appeal when you're sick with flu. The argument that the MW in question was so experienced she could evaluate wines without being able to smell them (while taking decongestants at the time) is spurious.

Removing the sense of smell from the equation really does transform any tasting into a blind one, although perhaps not quite in the way that producers paying close to R1,000 to enter their wines into the competition would appreciate. Richard Dawkins' blind watchmaker of his eponymous novel about evolution kicks up a stink: four genes are associated with the sense of sight while more than one thousand are necessary to nail down smell.

Smell is the least developed of our senses and is the only one that gets piped directly into the centres of the brain that deal with memory and emotion. The others get censored by the thalamus and are then passed on to the cortex for further processing.

Our human sensory world is dominated by the visual, and even taste gets a better press than smell: restaurant menus surrender to paroxysms of delight when describing the flavours of a dish, but are coy on the subject of smell.

How does smell work? A recent new theory on the physical mechanics of smell, *The Secret of Scent* (Faber and Faber, 2006) by Luca Turin, proposes that we recognise smells by sensing the vibration of molecules, rather than the shape of aromatic molecules, via a form of nasal Velcro. From a philosophical point of view this gives a warm and satisfying feeling, as those other two remote senses, sight and sound, also take place in the vibrational plane.

The lock and key hypothesis to explain smell was clearly never going to work unaided, as there are exactly 347 different human odour receptors, while we can typically differentiate many thousands of different smells. The vibration theory, however, is not the last word either, since research published in *Nature Neuroscience* in 2004 reported that volunteers could not distinguish between molecules with different atomic vibrations but the same shape. So while the scientific jury is still out considering its verdict, speculation on the mechanics of smell continues unabated.

One of the more intriguing claims in Turin's book is that at least one champagne producer adds an illegal scent 'to boost brand loyalty'. But while Turin's book is written by the scientist who did most of the heavy lifting and made the major breakthroughs, a more accessible book on the subject is *The Emperor of Scent* (Random House, 2003) by Chandler Burr. (The title anticipates *The Emperor of Wine* (Ecco, 2005), Elin McCoy's biography of Robert Parker, America's million-dollar nose.)

Burr is well qualified for the job of explicator: he's the first perfume critic at *The New York Times*, with a bi-monthly column, 'Scent Notes', which rates perfumes on a *Platter's* five-star scale (also sighted, like *Platter's*). Judging by his column, the world of perfume is even more highly charged than the observations of a fevered wine anorak. Fashion designer Tom Ford is quoted as 'dreaming of a perfume that smelled like fresh cherry wood licked by a green-hot oxygen fire in a Balinese temple'.

Burr demonstrates a clean pair of winespeak heels himself. In a column called 'Men Smelling Badly' he notes:

> 'Osmanthe Yunnan smells like a field of hay: you inhale summer sunlight, perhaps some dry straw, clover and honey. It also smells (and there's no other way to describe it) bizarrely more human than that – as if these earthly delights had been caught on the sweaty skin of the young man harvesting that field. Jean-Claude Ellena, the Hermès perfumer, has taken this complex tonality and built out of it a scent the way a master carpenter turns raw oak into a perfect, linear, quietly masculine chest of drawers. The experience of smelling it is like that of listening to an orchestra tuning up: dozens of instruments intent on finding their own perfect balance, a scattering of notes, and then the composer taps the podium.'

All the usual winespeak bases are gracefully covered: gratuitous anthropomorphism, linearity, musical analogues while dropping in the name of the perfumier in the process.

Turin clears up many misconceptions and makes some important points, like why smokers are often more precise nosers than non-smokers. The late Stellenbosch Farmers' Winery managing director Ronnie Melck was a famous puffer and ace taster; Anthony Hamilton Russell is no slouch in the sniffing, swirling and spitting stakes in spite of a serious Hoyo de Monterey habit. Bernd Philippi was likewise a sharp-tasting Marlboro man for decades.

Turin claims that the carbon monoxide in cigarette smoke totally blocks the enzyme cytochrome P450, which breaks down smell molecules, with the result that they persist in the nose, improving smell. All music to the ears of Johann Rupert, South Africa's king of tobacco, with a much anticipated and headily aromatic L'Ormarins red blend waiting in the wings.

The second shibboleth blown up faster than a Gauteng ATM is the idea that smell is primarily to do with sex. Turin notes:

> 'Smell is not about sex, contrary to popular belief, it's about food and protection from decaying, poisonous things that can hurt you.'

This doesn't explain Somerset Maugham's anecdote on the success that the fat and homely H.G. Wells enjoyed with women:

'I once asked one of his mistresses what especially attracted her to him. I expected her to say his acute mind and sense of fun. Not at all. She said that his body smelt of honey.'

Another intriguing idea is that smells are objectively real. This would mean that the olfactory experience of MWs and civilians alike to a glass of Shiraz is exactly the same, although acuity does decline with advancing age – 50 seems to be the threshold to the slopes of anosmia. This could explain the variability of blind tasting results featuring mature tasters: most local ones are on the angel's side of 50. As Turin notes, 'Oh, to hell with "expertise" – it doesn't exist!' A sentiment shared by many unhappy wine show participants.

But perhaps the most intriguing feature of the new theory is the accommodation for superposition of smells. Turin explains that the aroma (and hence taste) of caraway consists of mint and cabonyl (aka acetone or nail varnish remover). So blending a minty The- lema Merlot with a rustic Jacobsdal Pinotage should produce a spicy Cape Blend with a distinct aniseed flavour. Which opens up endless blending possibilities – designer wines assembled from a fragrant palate of aromatic ingredients.

Reviewing *The Secret of Scent* in *The Guardian*, Alex Butterworth concludes that 'Turin is a true amateur whose conspicuous sincerity is refreshing in an age of constructed passions and marketing.' Just the kind of decongestant South African wine needs to clear the pipes clogged by conflicts of interest and terminal cultural cringe.

While a clear nose is a necessary prerequisite for choosing wine by smell, La Kovalyov's indisposition did have its funny side. Mar- cel Proust was something of an expert on taste and smell. He was also a snob and hypochondriac, whose lucky break arrived in 1919 when he caught a head cold from the British ambassador, Lord Derby. A friend noted: 'The English cold lasted all spring, which gave him a thousand opportunities to mention Lord Derby, which he liked to do often.' The flu of La Kovalyov was clearly a direct descendant of Lord Derby's cold among fashionable Cape anoraks. A photograph of her at Chamonix in Franschhoek, tissue firmly clutched in hand, was given pride of place on the homepage of the website *Grape* (www.grape.org.za) for days.

All things considered, Proust would have made a formidable wine judge along the lines of a refined version of Robert Parker, but, thankfully, wine competitions were unknown in the Paris of the roaring twenties. As indeed they remain to this day.

And there is a strange South African connection to Proust. The love of his life was a young chauffeur-cum-mechanic called Alfred Agostinelli who would take his employer on country jaunts at night, shining his headlights so the great soul could admire the roses.

Could Alfred be related to Michele Agostinelli who arrived in South Africa in 1940 as an Italian prisoner of war? Fairview owner Charles Back credits Michele Agostinelli with establishing the burgeoning Fairview cheese business and remembers him in a range of exciting wines made from classic Italian varietals, like Sangiovese and Barbera.

The cheese maker certainly had a happier life than his name-sake, who died when he crashed the plane that Proust had bought him into the Mediterranean off Antibes on his second solo flight. Unable to swim, he clung to the wreckage, making pitiful gestures for help, but drowned before rescuers could reach him.

As Stevie Smith wrote, 'not waving but drowning'.

The Boer War continued by other means

The UK remains the most important market by far for South African wine exports. But the competition is stiff and not all the UK commentators are on message.

One of the more understandable concepts of the late French philosopher Jacques Derrida is the notion of 'unconditional hospitality'. Simply stated, if you invite someone into your home, you shouldn't try to dictate their behaviour. This lesson in deconstruction was brought home to WOSA by UK wine writer and co-chairman of the International Wine Challenge, Tim Atkin.

Brought to South Africa twice in 2006 by WOSA, Atkin enthused about South African whites, noting that 'the Cape is producing some of the top Sauvignons in the world at the moment'. Yet when he released his top 36 wines for summer in *The Observer*, alas, none made the list.

Reds came in for an even rougher ride. In an article entitled 'Is the Cape waking up to the dawn of the red?' in the July 2007 edition of *Wine & Spirit* magazine, Atkin calls South Africa 'the worst of the major New World wine-producing nations' for red wine.

The strapline continues: 'Its whites are vastly superior, says Tim Atkin, but South Africa may at last be improving on its reds if a recent tasting is anything to go by.' The largely negative tone conjures up images from the seventies American horror film *Dawn of the Dead*, released internationally as *Zombi*.

As New York Yankee catcher Yogi Berra said, this judgement – which Atkins admits is a personal point of view – is déjà vu all over again. The same point had been made more elegantly the previous month in *The Financial Times* by Jancis Robinson and echoed by Michael Fridjhon in *The Weekender*.

The red rot seems to have started at the International Wine

Challenge in London (Atkin and Fridjhon both co-chairmen), at which South Africa won 12 gold medals, with eight going to whites (and stickies) and only four to reds. It then spread like the plague in *Dawn of the Dead* to Paarl and Fridjhon's Toasty Show.

Atkin hilariously describes 'many South African domestic wine writers' as 'parochial, barely qualified fan[s] with a typewriter' (no doubt I'm one of these). But while I'm the last to defend the widely discredited circus of wine shows and those South African wine writers with more conflicts of interest than a chameleon sitting on a box of Smarties, it is worth pointing out that other forums do not subscribe to this white-power agenda in South African wines. Quite the opposite, actually.

Starting with sighted assessments and leaving out dessert wines and ports, the Platter's pundits from Mount Anorak sat on the fence for the 2008 edition of their guide, with whites and reds scoring seven five-star stunners each. Including all wines, the reds have it by a margin of 12 to 9. And who knows, if slow electrons had not derailed the submission of three wines from Waterford for Platter's five-star tasting (including the flagship Jem red blend), perhaps the reds would have taken it.

But then the problem with Platter's five-star tasting is that, while it is done blind, wines are nominated sighted. Even an associate editor was moved to comment that he did not agree with 'the taster who decided that Sadie's Columella 2005 wasn't even worth considering as a five-star candidate'. Which, if successful, would have been another vote for red.

When it comes to blind tastings, reds are more convincing. Results from the Michelangelo International Wine Awards (the second largest South African wine show after Veritas) reveal that of the 30 double gold medals dished out, over half went to red wines, including trophy for best wine of show.

Whites lagged, with six double golds. Dessert wines, brandies and Jerepigos made up the balance. This was no triumph of local flavour: the Michelangelo organisers take great pains to note that 'unlike other South African wine competitions, the Michelangelo International Wine Awards is judged by a panel consisting of international judges plus only one local judge'. A triumph of cultural cringe.

What's more, if you leave out the many regional trophies, the Decanter World Wine Awards dished out 80 per cent of their South African gold medals to reds in 2006 – exactly the same proportion as the 2007 Concours Mondial de Bruxelles, with 17 red golds out of 21.

Closer to home, the Swiss International Airlines Wine Awards, under the chairmanship of another UK wine authority and founder of the International Wine Challenge, Robert Joseph, gave 20 of their 28 gold gongs to reds. Of course, there could have been many more reds entered than whites – as was hopefully the case at the Syrah du Monde competition where South Africa bagged seven of 34 golds awarded against Australia's mingy two. In fact, South Africa came second only to France and was, therefore, the best New World Syrah performer. A further inconvenient truth for the Atkin white-power thesis.

Sticking with American opinion, US pundit James Molesworth is clearly in the red corner. Writing in *Wine Spectator*, he makes the point that Stellenbosch, the heart of quality South African wine production by any measure, has Cabernet-based blends as its strong suit, while Paarl and the Swartland are best for Syrah and Rhône varieties. Indeed, the *Spectator's* best rated South African wine ever is Eben Sadie's Columella 2005, a blend of Syrah and Mourvèdre.

Perhaps Atkin's dislike of South African reds comes from his experience at the 2007 outing of the International Wine Challenge. Few premium South African producers take this show seriously, however, after controversial results in 2006 left many highly regarded South African reds from icon producers like Vergelegen and Meerlust as naked as an apple-chomping Adam, without even a fig leaf commendation award for wines that won golds in other contemporaneous tourneys.

In fact, how seriously should one take London wine competitions when a wine entered three times (by the producer, importer and retailer) to one show managed to win a bronze, silver and gold medal *for the same wine.* To paraphrase Nigel Andrews writing in *The Financial Times* on the subject of Oscars, 'these handouts are given by the mad to the glad'.

While Mr Atkin is entitled to his opinions, his attack on South African wine writers in the same story raised a few hackles. Approached for his reaction, Cassie du Plessis, editor of *Wine-Land* and *Fynproe*, was the soul of diplomacy:

> 'Our South African wine writing colleagues represent the whole spectrum, from pretty ordinary to very smart and informed, with most hovering safely around the middle. Then, many supposed wine writers are really wine business or lifestyle writers, with few focusing seriously on wine quality and style. Unfortunately, there are some of these who don't do much more than rework statements from PR companies and who slavishly hang on to the lips of some outspoken/influential wine personalities who they can safely support.

> 'The sad reality is that we have hundreds of wineries who vie for the attentions of a handful of writers and publications who they hope can swing the scale in the face of oversupply and market domestic stagnancy. And there's no professional association guarding the standards and ethics of South African wine writing. It's just about a free for all – with many writers having to juggle clashing interests to make a decent living.'

Hardly a ringing endorsement. If not the South African wine press, however, then who will blow the trumpet for the hundreds of wineries out there? Atkin has a solution: 'In the absence of a more robust domestic media . . . South Africa needs informed criticism from overseas.'

From a publication such as *Decanter*, presumably. As the magazine's website modestly proclaims, '*Decanter* magazine is – quite simply – the world's best wine magazine. Sold in 92 countries, *Decanter* is required reading for everyone with an interest in wine – from connoisseurs to amateur enthusiasts.'

A sentiment shared by readers of *WINE*. An online poll reported in that magazine's September 2007 edition confirms that two-thirds of respondents name *Decanter* as the international magazine they rate most highly.

Through the Decanter World Wine Awards and in particular the person of consultant editor Steven Spurrier, a judge at the controversial 2007 Toasty Show and wine selector for Singapore Airlines, *Decanter* has an influence on South African wine well above its local circulation figures.

Which could explain the blizzard of angry phone calls and letters from lawyers when www.winenews.co.za reported on the allegations of Gaetano Manti, editor of Italian wine magazine *Il Mio Vino* in the June 2007 edition that *Decanter* offers 'stories' for sale. *Decanter* editor Guy Woodward confirms that 'advertorials are commonplace in lifestyle magazines. We carry them occasionally, and they are always marked as promotional or advertising pages.'

Although obviously not flagged clearly enough to avoid confusion among Italian producers or *Il Mio Vino*. As I discovered when I posed a simple question to Manti:

Q: Is it acceptable to sell advertorial?

A: It is not. Let me explain why. If we go to Webster's Dictionary *we find the following definition of the word advertorial: 'An advertisement that is written and presented in the style of an editorial or journalistic report'.*

In my book this means cheating on the readers. No wonder in Italy advertisers have given themselves a code of conduct that explicitly prohibits placing ads that have the look and feel of editorial. The reality of the

matter is that no reputable magazine would ever accept selling and publishing so-called advertorials. I know Decanter claims that advertorials
are commonplace in lifestyle magazines. They should be talking just about
themselves, since I can name a dozen lifestyle magazines published by the
same company that publishes Decanter (IPC Media) that would never
sell and publish advertorials. The fact that IPC allows its wine magazine
to do what other magazines of the same publishing company would never
dare do should say a lot about how far the wine information industry
has gone into unethical territory.

Q: Decanter threatened legal action and Winenews withdrew the story.
Did you have the same experience?

A: So far, we have not heard from anybody. What I wrote in my magazine is true and fully documented by Decanter's own rate card. This is
a free world and Decanter is certainly free to take any action they want.
It is going to be extremely easy for us to prove that what we described is
100 per cent accurate.

Q: Strange. Guy Woodward, Decanter editor, told me they were 'taking
legel [sic] action' against you a month ago. Is there a code of conduct for
Italian wine journalists – are commercial contacts with producers toler-
ated, for example?

A: Italian journalists are subject to a very strict code of conduct that
explicitly prohibits commercial contacts with producers and explicitly
prohibits journalists from writing editorial paid by advertisers. I can't
tell how strict wine journalists are in complying with their code of conduct. I just know that in our magazine the code is applied in a very
strict way.

What I know for sure is that when I read in Decanter's rate card that
the cost of advertorials 'does include the work of the journalist or the
translation and the editing of an existing Italian text, the creative work

and the layout', then I am confronted with conduct that is definitively not acceptable by Italian standards. I do not know the British standards but I do know a number of reputable British journalists who would refuse to write for advertorials. How can one possibly write an advertorial paid for by a wine producer and then be totally unbiased when it comes to writing a real story about those wines?

Q: How about sighted tastings for wine guides. Can these give fair assessments?

A: A sighted tasting cannot possibly produce a fair assessment. This is the reason why we carry only blind tastings. As for Decanter and its policy of selling advertorials, I just wonder how their team can be fair and unbiased tasting sighted wines of producers that have paid for the text of the advertorials. Can we possibly believe that they would also be prepared to give bad ratings to the wines of such producers and publish the results in the magazine?

The annual Platter's Wine Guide is exhibit A in using sighted rather than blind tastings to rank wines, with the exception of the four-star stunners that are nominated sighted and then tasted blind with a simple 'yea' or 'nay' from a majority of tasters sufficient to clinch the rating.

Platter's blind vision

The sighted method that Platter's uses to rate wine is arguably the most contentious issue in South Africa, especially for producers, many of whom feel hard done by. The commercial consequences of a bad rating are just too costly for producers or commentators to ignore.

The five most expensive wines in South Africa (Vergelegen V; Ernie Els; Saxenburg Shiraz; Waterford Jem and Eben Sadie's Columella) have something in common: they all rate four-and-a-half stars in the 2008 edition of *Platter's Wine Guide*. A cynical interpretation would be that they were all proposed for five stars by one of the 15 Platter pundits, but failed to get the nod at the blind tasting. As wines are nominated sighted, this would be taken as further proof of research reported in the proceedings of the US National Academy of Sciences in January 2008 that the brain is a wine snob – thinking that a wine is expensive contributes to its enjoyment.

But this being South Africa, where nothing should be attributed to design which can be explained by incompetence, the truth gives even less comfort to wannabe first-growth producers. The last two wines failed to make the five-star tasting, despite Columella being the first South African wine to garner a classic (ie 95/100) rating from *Wine Spectator*.

Leaving out the Jem and Columella was a classic stuff-up. While such tribulations are a source of great mirth and hilarity to the industry and great copy for commentators, they are ultimately damaging to South African wine writing and writers and provide ammunition for critics like Atkin.

The problem with sighted tastings are twofold. Firstly, the 15 Platter pundits are partial. One is the chairman of a major producer; others are professional winemakers; others are retailers, while others earn money from producers in various capacities (the most controversial being offering tasting assessments for a hefty fee). All benefit from cordial relations with producers to support their habit of free samples and invitations to functions.

Such obvious conflicts of interest should be avoided at all costs. In some sense, every wine tasted sighted is either a friend or an enemy and this is reflected in the partial nature of the ratings accorded. Examples of the same wine with wildly different ratings are legion, but perhaps even more worrying are mediocre wines receiving unexpectedly high ratings, like Platter's four-and-a-half stars for Racetrack '06 Chenin, which came last in a WineLand blind tasting. The reverse is also common, like the widely tipped Lismore Chardonnay '06, which languishes at two-and-a-half stars.

Both wines were rated sighted by the same high-profile taster so the utility of the guide is easily checked by performing a calibration exercise on these two wines for yourself and seeing which you prefer. But in reality the result is that the ratings are unreliable.

Next, the other problem is that some producers have such towering reputations that it takes a masochist to publicly downgrade them because the taster's identity is revealed to the broader public and to the producer in particular. Would you really tell big Schalk Burger that his barrel-fermented Welbedacht Chenin is *kak*?

This points to a further problem. I was involved in a minor altercation with a producer concerning additives and was told: 'No, you've got it wrong, it was only the show tank that was affected.' How many Platter tanks and barrels are being made in a way to secure a score which is then applied consistently to the rest of the production? What ends up on the shelves is sometimes inferior stuff. This is exactly what happened in New Zealand in 2006 when a wine writer smelt figurative rat pie in a bottle of Wither Hills Sauvignon Blanc bought from a supermarket. A wine that he'd previously rated sky-high in a tasting for a magazine.

The solution to this Wither Hills phenomenon is simple: buy your own wine from a retailer. And Platters's should do the same. At R143 a copy and a circulation of 100,000, plus all the paid-for punts for places to stay and eat in the Winelands, surely the Platter machine is making enough money to pay for its tasting stock? Even notoriously mingey food magazines pay the bills for the meals in the restaurants they review. As one disgruntled producer told me: 'We paid to advertise our guesthouse in Platter's in the hope of getting a better rating for our wines – but then the reverse happened.'

While my criticism of Platter's is becoming a tad monotonous (not least for me) and the hysterical calls from the editor start to lose their appeal, I've no desire to play Samson and bring down the temple of Bacchus around my ears. Platter's is a national treasure and could become an even more valuable asset for South African wine. With one simple change – blind assessment – it can become an order of magnitude better and truly the best wine guide in the world, as it states on the cover.

After all, blind vision is the right thing to do if you feel compelled to attribute a score rather than rely on language to convey the message. James Laube wrote in the December 2007 issue of *Wine Spectator*:

> '*Wine Spectator* has always believed in blind tastings, in which the identity of a wine is not known. In practice, that means that tasters review wines in coherent flights in order to provide a context. They know the region, the vintage and the grape variety, if relevant, of the wines in a flight. But they do not know the producer or the price, two factors that hold the biggest sway in people's perceptions of quality.

> 'This is the fairest, most objective method of evaluating wines. It allows each wine to stand on its own merits, in context with its peers. And it eliminates any bias that might result from knowing the producer or price. Some people say they aren't influenced by this information, but many studies have shown that this kind of bias is almost impossible to eliminate.'

In the South African context, even knowing the region upfront may be problematic as there are definitely fashionable appellations (such as Stellenbosch and its various *bergs*: Helder, Simons, etc) and unfashionable ones. This piece of information is perhaps also best left undisclosed to tasters.

With several producers asking to be excluded from the guide, a resolution to the sighted versus blind debate will probably be decided when the guide reaches a tipping point and loses its catholic reach. Meanwhile, the last word in the *Decanter* advertorial debate came from an unlikely source.

With Afrikaans the lingua franca of South African wine producers, the whole affair became much more relevant when George Claassen raised several ethical issues in *Die Burger* concerning wine writing. Former Professor of Journalism at the University of Stellenbosch, Claassen is ombudsman for the newspaper and his comments under the headline 'when the wine in wine journalism turns to vinegar' pull no punches. He gets straight to the point. 'How much value can wine lovers attach to the ratings of wine publications and wine writers?' he asks, when he receives so many examples of unethical wine judging and marketing. The one he presents is of a so-called blind tasting at a restaurant on Table Mountain, with a group of wine connoisseurs and writers judging bottles from which the brand labels had been removed, although the back labels were 'conveniently' still visible.

Cars and wine are the two areas of journalism that Claassen accuses of being run unethically, with advertorials – 'one of the biggest evils of journalism' – the main problem. He then goes on to quote an unnamed local pundit alleging that R10,000 will put a product on the cover of a publication in which paid-for comment is often passed off as editorial.

Ten grand seems to be the going rate. This was also the monthly payment one winery owner told me he makes to a journalist for 'marketing strategy advice'. (He was planning to halve the amount after being left out of a benchmark tasting arranged by the writer.) A figure ten times larger was the annual retainer one winemaker reported his company paid another hack.

Such conflicts of interest of certain published pundits make a mockery of transparency and devalue the South African winespeak currency.

Claassen then looks at the state of play outside South Africa and moves on to the story to which *Decanter* objected that appeared on www.winenews.co.za. Entitled 'When everything has a price', I wrote it in response to complaints by several local winemakers about the coverage of the Decanter World Wine Awards in the magazine, where the form in which results are printed is a function of how much one pays. With over one thousand entries in 2008, the Decanter World Wine Awards are up there with Veritas and the Michelangelo International Wine Awards as the most important wine shows on the South African calendar.

Clearly, everything does have a price: my story was removed from the *Winenews* website after legal threats. *Decanter* ignored *Il Mio Vino*, however, 'in all likelihood because a story in Italian would attract nowhere near as many readers as one in English on the Internet', Claassen concludes.

With Claassen now having translated my Italian translation into Afrikaans and posted it on the *Die Burger* site (http://www.die-burger.com/Stories/Opinion/Columns/15.0.3276491052.aspx), the potential readership may be smaller by several orders of magnitude, but the effect is unlikely to be as diminished.

Atkin is not alone in the UK wine press in harbouring an antipathy to South African reds. Jane MacQuitty can usually be relied on to put in the boot, as she did the week after the Rugby World Cup in 2007.

BIG, BURLY BRUISERS

Then there are the pundits who write off the whole category.

The last time the Springboks won the Rugby World Cup, the Kiwis complained of food poisoning. This time it was rubber in the wine, which gave the boks a bouncy advantage in line-out and scrum. South Africans don't come much more burly than Schalk Burger, unless you include his dad, 'Big' Schalk, who owns Welbe-dacht estate in Wellington. Welbedacht Shiraz grapes possess such Michelin terroir they bounced Marc Kent and his Boekenhouts-kloof 2005 Syrah all the way to Diners Club Winemaker of the Year. Jonny Wilkinson and his mates stood no chance at all.

Schalk could have been one of the 'Burly South Africans' that 'Calamity' Jane MacQuitty had in mind, when she reported in *The Times* (UK) the week after the Springbok victory that 'South Africa has yet to tame its red wine's peculiar burnt rubber and dirt odour'.

The words 'yet to' in the subheadline remind one of 'when did you stop beating your wife?'. MacQuitty's assumption is that there is a problem, a position contested by the response of WOSA, which told the *Sunday Times* (South Africa) that 'MacQuitty was entitled to her view, but statistics showed that consumers across the world think otherwise and rate South Africa's wines highly.'

The 'peculiar burnt rubber odour' that set the olfactory papillae of *The Times* pundit vibrating may undoubtedly be real for her, but if she smelt it in a West-End movie house while watching a press pre-view of *Mondovino*, would she shout 'fire!' in a crowded cinema?

The sales force of Australian, New Zealand, Californian, Chilean, etc wine producers would be fools if they don't bring her incendiary concerns to the notice of those who buy their wines for the many restaurants, gastropubs and supermarkets of Blighty. If you bear in mind that only now are sales of Austrian wine recovering from the 1985 antifreeze scandal, the power of a bad wine press should not be underestimated.

What was unusual (just as much so as the England 12-10 semi-final victory over the Wallabies) was that MacQuitty picked up rubber whiffs in 'a run of the country's flagship reds', at the Octo-ber WOSA Megatasting in London. 'Priced from £16 to £40 a bottle . . . mostly Bordeaux-inspired blends, and half of them dis-played this unpleasant taint.'

While burnt rubber is perhaps a note you might expect to encounter in Pinotage (indeed, she goes on to recommend 'Diemersfontein's masterly 2006 Pinotage' to her readers, 'with its sweet, *burnt*, heavy, peppery fruit'), warm-climate Shiraz or in wines made from the Roobernet grape, to find it in the expensive Bordeaux blends presented is a worry worthy of further investigation.

Which is starting to happen in fact. South African UK-based Master of Wine Lynne Sherriff is quoted as confirming the existence of a 'burnt rubber aromatics problem'. Sherriff confirms that WOSA is speaking to researchers at the University of Stellenbosch to try and nail down the origin and extent of the problem.

Sherriff reports:

> 'The issue was raised in *Harpers* recently, but it is not as though all of the trade is talking about this. It is more of a curiosity aspect, with certain journos/members of the trade saying – what is that "burnt rubber/slightly medicinal/iodine/ tapenade/olive paste/savoury note" that sometimes crops up in South African reds?'

A storm in a wine spittoon is usually vicious but brief, thanks to the shallow draught of the container. Wine columns and columnists thrive on hyperbole and exaggeration. The last *cause célèbre* was Brett (Brettanomyces contamination), which miraculously cleared up when wineries threatened to sue those irresponsible gurus who loudly started detecting it in every Shiraz they nosed.

That said, André Shearer, the most successful importer of South African wines into the United States, admits:

> 'I sadly do believe that many of South Africa's wines have a phenolic "unripeness" which I believe is at the root (pardon the pun) of the problem, and may be the reason some find this "burnt rubber" characteristic. Surprisingly few producers even taste it . . . it is a familiarity issue.'

This echoes MacQuitty's contention: 'South Africans themselves are tolerant of their country's distinctive red wine characteristic, and even British merchants specialising in Cape wines often just don't see it.'

In the line-up tasted by MacQuitty were such icons as De Toren Fusion V; Rustenberg John X Merriman; Kanonkop; Paul Sauer and Tokara Red. According to Shearer, these 'all fare very well here in the United States, receiving top 90+ scores from *Wine Spectator*, or Stephen Tanzer. I do not believe these wines have any aspect of "burnt rubber".'

Neither did the Beyerskloof Field Blend 2003 that I had at lunch at Assaggi, nor the Spar Country Cellars Quintette 2005 – my current best buy. All this offers a simple solution for fire-averse palates: better screenings of wines selected for a public showcase.

Nevertheless, Shearer does go on to make the following points:

> 'South Africa will *never* reach the heights of even a "mini-Australia", given our inability to taste our own shortcomings. Furthermore, the US market will simply never commercially accept those wines, which is precisely why the United States is proving to have such a high barrier to entry for so many South African producers.

> 'That "funny, unripe red style" will never cut it. Thank God our exports are flourishing as we have been paying simple heed to that precise feedback from the US consumer over the 16 years we've been here . . . People in South Africa think I am trying to "Americanise" our style – that's not the case. Nobody really wants to drink unripe when they can drink ripe – it goes against the human taste bud!'

While Atkin may prefer South African whites, the reds have at least one *Dawn of the Dead*-type fan. In 2001, German cannibal Armin Meiwes cooked and ate Bernd Brandes, a manager at Siemens in

Berlin. *Stern* magazine reported that parts of Brandes were cooked 'with olive oil, garlic, pepper and nutmeg and eaten with sprouts, potatoes and a bottle of South African red wine on a festively decorated table'. A Platter's contribution on the tasting match is a real possibility.

Shearer's comments about phenolic ripeness raise an interesting point: could it be that Americans have different tastes to South Africans or Brits, preferring sweeter, riper styles of wine to those of more structure and grip? It would certainly explain the war of taste that periodically flares up on the other side of the Atlantic.

A TRANSATLANTIC WAR OF TASTE

South Africa is not the only country in the sights of the chattering classes from the world of UK vino. Another former colony also comes in for some stick, on the odd occasion.

Fred Astaire sang phonetically: 'You say "toemayto", I say "toemarto" . . . let's call the whole thing off' and this seems to be the message the British wine empire is sending to its American cousins across the pond. While simplified American spelling (color, thru, sulfur, etc) makes lexicographic sense, when it comes to simplifying wine, the *goût américain* (fruit-driven; big alcohol; obvious wood; residual sugar) is seriously getting up the noses of British *snifferati*.

Hardly had Elin McCoy's modestly titled *The Emperor of Wine: the rise of Robert M. Parker and the reign of American taste* (Ecco, 2005) hit the bookshelves, than Britain's doyen of winespeak, Hugh Johnson, was wading in with accusations of absolutism in his autobiography *Wine: a life uncorked* (University of California Press, 2006):

> 'Taste in the past was largely a matter of harmless fashion. In American hands it feels more like a moral crusade. Robert Parker deals in absolutes, and castigates those he sees as backsliders . . . Imperial hegemony lives in Washington and

the dictator of taste in Baltimore. His opinions go around
the world at Internet speed. And not only do they travel infi-
nitely further and faster, but they have become, as it were,
enforceable.'

Take, for example, Parker's attack on Jancis Robinson. Her offence
was to trash a wine, Château Pavie 2003, that this prince of palates
had anointed. Robinson was challenged to a 'celebrity death match'
by His Bobness. While disputing with a lawyer (Parker's previous
profession) is always a dodgy pastime, this 'death match' would see
the loser 'drowned in a vat of St-Emilion *garagiste* brew'.

A quite appropriate resolution to *L'Affaire Pavie,* which has caused
the largest splash in the global wine spittoon since the Austrians
abandoned antifreeze in making their delicate and elegant whites.

Château Pavie is one of Bordeaux's biggest names and owned by
the larger-than-life Parisian supermarket tycoon turned wine aristo-
crat Gérard Perse. Jancis Robinson's considered opinion of Perse's
plonk was characteristically terse:

> 'Completely unappetising overripe aromas. Why? Porty sweet.
> Port is best from the Douro not St-Emilion. Ridiculous wine
> more reminiscent of late-harvest Zinfandel than a red Bor-
> deaux with its unappetising green notes.'

Of the same wine, Parker sang from a different hymn sheet:

> 'An off the chart effort . . . a wine of sublime richness, miner-
> ality, delineation, and nobleness. Representing the essence of
> one of St-Emilion's greatest terroirs, the limestone and clay
> soils were perfect for handling the torrid heat of 2003. Inky/
> purple to the rim, it offers up provocative aromas of minerals,
> black and red fruits, balsamic vinegar, licorice, and smoke.
> It traverses the palate with extraordinary richness as well as
> remarkable freshness and definition.'

Jancis Robinson scored it 12/20, a rating that the *Wine Spectator* notes, 'implies that the wine is not acceptable'.

Parker scored it 98/100, while a Grand Jury Européen blind tasting placed it first out of 160 Bordeaux wines, according to *Decanter.*

It's clearly a clash of tastes. Hugh Johnson had a similar experience. Faced with a bunch of Parker high 90s, he said that 'they were wines for cigar smokers – which I didn't intend as a compliment'. The process of making a Parker hi-pointer is 'mainly self-denial. First you accept a tiny crop: concentration is all.' To fine-tune the reduced juice, 'massage with tiny bubbles . . . to settle its molecules in patterns agreeable to a discerning tongue'. Add strong aromas with new oak: 'Even give it new barrels twice to make sure no-one misses the smell.'

Johnson despairs of the result: 'The alchemy of oak seems to clog the wine's pores, glaze it like gesso on a picture frame.' It tastes like a Teflon pan: 'I feel frustrated: why can't I taste the fruit – or the terroir?' For Johnson this is the antithesis of claret, 'whose genius lies in making great light wine – light on the palate, light on the spirits, light on the constitution'.

This clash of styles even made it into the pages of the *London Review of Books* in an article entitled 'Hedonistic Fruit Bombs'. Written by Steven Shapin, Harvard professor in the Department of the History of Science and one-time member of the North Edinburgh Wine Tasting Society, it compares the Pavie dispute with the US War on Terror.

Parker plays the role of President Bush: both are 'loathed' by 'old Europe'. 'The power both are seen to wield is as coercive as it is crude and clumsy.' Shapin quotes Parker protégé and *garagiste* Jean-Luc Thunevin, of Château de Valandraud, who describes the Europeans as 'reactionaries' who have 'the aesthetics of sour grapes' and behave like 'ayatollahs of terroir'.

While differing opinions of Pavie are ultimately a matter of taste, the point that Shapin quotes Parker on, namely that critics should pay their own way, with 'no free bottles; no complimentary air travel; no cosy guest rooms' is pretty hard to dispute. By Parker's lights, British wine commentators are compromised pundits, with Hugh Johnson in the first carriage of the gravy train.

As William Echikson notes in *Noble Rot* (Norton, 2005), Johnson is 'on Château Latour's board, under contract with the mail-order London *Sunday Times* wine club, consults for the Royal Tokay Wine Company in Hungary, and sold his own ranges of glassware and wine paraphernalia'. Which makes his opinion on wines suspect to those of a puritanical persuasion.

Johnson's Latour gig, alas, came to an end after he was fired by the new owner (another supermarket mogul, François Pinault) for non-attendance at board meetings (three a year: one at Latour and two in Paris, 'at the owner's convenience and not always with a great deal of notice', according to Echikson).

Johnson owns an Elizabethan country pile, Saling Hall, in Essex; a flat in London (St James's); farm in France (Bourbonnais); vine-yard in Tokay and a comfortable berth in every winemaking appellation on the planet.

Still, Johnson is a very good writer indeed and his description of an Aussie sparkling Shiraz as 'a fat old man dressed up as a fairy' is certainly more amusing than the score out of 100 that Parker would bestow. In fact, his ability to use 'crystalline', 'penetrating', 'poised', 'luxurious', 'fragrant' and 'foghorn' in a single sentence to describe an Australian wine confirms Johnson as a connoisseur. The kind of man the world's first gourmet, Brillat-Savarin, probably had in mind when he noted that 'true connoisseurship was possible only for those who had the right sort and number of taste buds'.

Scottish empiricist David Hume called such connoisseurs Masters of Taste (hence the 'qualification', Master of Wine, I suspect). He noted that many of them were 'a great inconvenience' to be around. While a public cat fight between two such high-profile Masters of Taste makes an amusing sideshow on a slow news day, there is also an important message for South African wine and its obsession with awards.

Assuming that Jancis Robinson's bottle was not faulty, the two expert opinions could not have been more different in this case. This could go a long way to explaining why the same wine is praised to the rafters by one tasting panel and sinks without trace at another.

Perhaps the last word on *L'Affaire Pavie* should go to Monsieur Perse, who has penned an impassioned three-page letter on the subject: 'Never did I imagine that trying to make the best wines possible could elicit such virulent criticism and even vicious personal attacks.'

He goes on to denounce those British wine critics who wanted to turn the clock back to when 'Bordeaux wines were made the way they should be'. Presumably between 1152 and 1435 when Bordeaux belonged to the English crown.

PS
Having given the last word to M Perse, it was rudely snatched away by economic reality. Seems that – high Parker score or not – Perse set the price so high that very little of the Pavie was sold.

Winespeak

If Noseweek *(great name for a wine magazine, but, alas, it's the South African version of UK satirical weekly* Private Eye*) ever initiated a 'Pseud's Corner', there would be no shortage of submissions.*

Those semioticians and philologists who reckon that most English speakers have a vocabulary of 10,000 words can't have included wine writers in their sample. Even Shakespeare, at 29,066 different words, pales in comparison to the flights of fancy conjured up by winespeak wordsmiths. In addition to being a fertile breeding ground for yeasts and diverse bacteria, the fermented fruit of the vine is an inspiration for countless new words.

Perhaps the best example comes from the language spoken at the southern tip of Argentina. The inhabitants of Tierra del Fuego have a word, *mamihlapinatapai*, which the *Guinness Book of Records* calls the hardest word in the world to define. It means 'two people looking at one another without speaking; each hoping the other will offer to do something both parties desire but neither is willing to do'. Wine lovers will immediately seize on it to describe that moment when your eyes catch those of your drinking partner and you realise you both know that the wine in your glass is corked.

It would have come in handy the last time South African Airways selected champagne in France in those salad days when Coleman Andrews ran the airline, accountants were grounded and Michael Fridjhon was the airline's wine consultant, billeted in the Michelin three-star auberge Boyer les Crayères in Reims. *Mamihlapinatapai* would have been the word with which to shout down the snooty sommelier as he topped up the claret with a corked second bottle – a feat he managed twice at the same dinner.

The 250th anniversary of the publication of the first major English dictionary did not go unnoticed. Henry Hitchings' fascinating biography cum philology, *Dr Johnson's Dictionary – Defining the world* (Farrar, Straus & Giroux, 2005) was published to mark the event. Dr Johnson, a quintessential British eccentric with an unreasonable hatred of cucumbers ('a cucumber should be well sliced, and dressed with pepper and vinegar, and then thrown out, as good for nothing') and a cat called Hodge, which he fed on oysters. Prone to hugging his publisher's lime tree while deep in thought, Johnson was also a collector of orange peel and would expel his breath in snorts, like a whale.

A 'hardened and shameless tea-drinker' who often ate seven or eight peaches before breakfast, Johnson was also an encyclopedic genius and cultural steeplejack who almost single-handedly compiled a resource that is a goldmine for winespeakers.

Some examples should make the point. While 'duck fart' is an endearing Australian colloquialism used to describe the pungent barnyard aromas given off by ripe Shiraz, Dr Johnson's 'anatiferous' (relating to ducks) is a far more genteel term. Or rather than being over the hill, an oxidised wine could be said to have started to 'australise' (head south). One with a short finish may be said to 'vade', while another with a strong nose could be criticised for excessive 'effumability'.

Johnson himself was rather partial to a Bishop, 'a cant word for a mixture of wine, oranges and sugar', Hitchings explains, which he would match with a whole roasted orange. And while he had good things to say about brandy ('claret is the liquor for boys; port, for men; but he who aspires to be a hero . . . must drink brandy'), the distiller who makes the stuff is put down as 'one who makes and sells pernicious and inflammatory spirits'.

But perhaps the finest contribution to early winespeak comes from Archibald 'Horrible' Campbell, an eighteenth-century ship's purser of famous ugliness. Moved to pen a put-down of Johnson as a grandiloquent bore, his words sound like the instructions to judges at a pompous wine competition: 'Expulse all agglomerated asperities lest they obthurate the porches of your intelligence with the adscititious excrement of critical malevolence.'

One of the most gifted wine wordsmiths still plying his trade, despite the minor irritation of losing his column, is Malcolm Gluck. A frequent visitor to South Africa, he can always be counted on to raise a stink.

MALCOLM GLUCK

Perhaps the most controversial UK wine writer, with a lot to say about South African wine.

When Malcolm Gluck and *The Guardian* parted ways in 2004, South Africa lost her best wine writer. A champion of so-called supermarket wines (the UK wine retail channel handling the overwhelming majority of South African imports), Gluck and his 'Superplonk' column cut through the forests of pretentious twaddle of winespeak with its wafts of dense cassia and capsicum and concentrated on value for money. Although that said, *Gluckspeak* is not without an idiosyncratic style.

A frequent guest of WOSA, Gluck would typically start off a feature on the South African wine scene berating the South African Airways first-class experience, before moaning about having to hang around Cape Town International for a tardy WOSA apparatchik to arrive. But at least with Mr Gluck, the verbal cartoon sketches more than make up for all the moaning.

His thumbnail of Boekenhoutskloof and Porcupine Ridge winemaker Marc Kent is a case in point: 'Mr Kent looks like the sort of hippie I lived near in Greenwich Village in 1969 and he is just as affable. Nothing disagreeable seems to nest in his beard.'

Facial hair fascinates the clean-shaven Gluck. He described the mustachioed prophet of Pinotage, Beyers Truter, as 'looking like an Amsterdam diamond merchant', while the pied piper of Paarl goats, with his Goats Do Something Outrageous brand, Charles Back, is proud owner of a 'supine baby porcupine on his upper lip which passes for a mustache [and] has been superbly trained and

only twitches when its master does'. Which is quite often, as Back
is the most dynamic wine personality in the Winelands.

Again, regally hirsute Hermanus winemaker Peter Finlayson, of
Bouchard Finlayson fame, has 'measured aplomb, deportment,
and [the] head of the Duke of Kent or if this seems extravagant
then the Duke's equerry', while clean-shaven Simon Barlow from
Rustenberg 'has the cheerful and gently chubby mien – and indeed
the moniker – of an English provincial bank manager of the 1960s:
keen to lend you money once he's established your bona fides,
which you find you provide without being aware of it'.

Indeed, Gluck is definitely onto something, as facial topiary is a
definitive feature of South African wine – probably on account of
Bacchus being portrayed classically in a beard and very little else.
The 'Full Furry Monty' is a signature look of writers as diverse as
yours truly; Dave 'Professor Dumbledore' Hughes; Graham 'Robinson Crusoe' Howe and Michael 'Mephistopheles' Fridjhon – and
Clark Gable mustaches sported by winemakers like Charles Hop-
kins and Jacques Borman.

Young Turks Adi Badenhorst (formerly of Rustenberg) and Bot
River roving winemaker Niels Verburg are more daring, both having been seen in exotic 'porno beards'. Which is quite appropriate
for the latter on the basis of Gluck's description of Niels: 'Given
a black suit and tie [he] would pass for one of the more terrifying
bouncers to be seen outside West London nightclubs.' His erstwhile
boss, Jayne Beaumont, of the eponymous winery, 'appears jolly as
a headmistress at end of term time'. Flagstone's Bruce Jack meanwhile 'exudes the red-cheeked authority of a scoutmaster'.

Over the hill in Elgin, this generation's pioneer of viticulture in
this cool climate valley, Paul Cluver, plays the patriarchal part: 'A
tall figure with the steady dignity and humble, pale, interiorised
features of a monastery archivist.'

In addition to wine reviews, Gluck is a fount of free advice. Like
his recommendation that Cape first-growth estate Meerlust, then
involved in legal action against confusingly named Franschhoek

estate Meerrust, change its name to 'Uitgelate Hormone Estate' (rampant hormones estate), as he finds the current name, Meerlust, 'so unsubtle'. Although with pronunciation an issue for UK consumers, Gluck's advice is less than useful in that department.

Just when South African winemakers thought that Gluck was as permanently off the air as the Goon Show or Monty Python, up he popped in *Harpers*, the UK wine trade industry magazine, with a blast against WOSA's biodiversity initiative that seeks to conflate South Africa's diverse wine styles with the diversity of our animal and plant ecology.

Gluck describes WOSA's claim that the diverse 'Cape Floral Kingdom . . . makes it possible to produce an enormous range of wine styles across the price spectrum' as 'half-baked' and with 'such inanities' that he likens it to suffering from calenture, 'the delirium which affected thirsty eighteenth-century sailors in the tropics. It is a belief that the sea is a green field and the sufferer has only to lie down in it to find relief.'

My own reservations about the initiative are a stool with three legs, starting with a regrettable lack of originality. Manhattan wine importer Neal Rosenthal, hailed as 'the father of wine biodiversity' by Lawrence Osborne in his hilarious *The Accidental Connoisseur* (North Point Press, 2004), is already a champion of the incredible diversity of taste and styles in wines made from Italy's indigenous grapes, many of which have become extinct.

And why hire foreign marketing consultants – as WOSA did – like James Herrick, MD of the quirkily named, French-based Cuppa Cup Vineyards, to come up with an unoriginal marketing concept? It's a fat slap in the face for the recently established wine marketing MBA programme at the UCT Business School, where Michael Fridjhon pops up again as a visiting professor. But perhaps the UCT spin-doctors were off designing a marketing plan to save plunging French sales in the UK (fat chance).

What's more, biodiversity is a curious platform from which to promote the vine – a Mediterranean weed and invader species in the Cape Floral Kingdom. From an ecological point of view, *Vitis vinifera* arrived on the same boat as the hated Port Jackson, the invasive plant on whose eradication millions are spent each year, or the beautiful jacaranda trees that brighten up the streets of Pretoria and Johannesburg but which, once deceased, may not be replanted by municipal fiat.

Or the blue agave cactus from which dot.bomb billionaires are now making tequila in the Karoo (much to the irritation of Mexicans, who thought tequila was their tipple).

The arrival of vineyards in the Cape three centuries ago actually decreased biodiversity. Fynbos was ripped out to plant vines, other indigenous vegetation suffered through changed water usage and pesticides decimated insect populations. In waterlogged Franschhoek, so much sulphur is used to prevent rot in the vineyards that locals miss their friendly birds. It's an ironic state of affairs that grape farmers, having transformed their ecosystems, are today the only ones wealthy enough to initiate conservation endeavours in the undeveloped portions of their farms.

Commuters on the London Underground might agree with Gluck's anti-biodiversity stance if they noticed the R2.2 million worth of billboards filled with proteas and other colourful fynbos above a strapline, 'Diversity is in our Nature' – part of WOSA's biodiversity initiative. *Decanter* personality Steven Spurrier famously didn't, as he gleefully told *WINE* magazine in an interview in between judging at the Toasty Show that WOSA's campaign 'failed to register' with him, a comment that kicked the local spittoon into touch.

A cynic might assume that South Africa is now making wine from flowers (Pinotage from proteas; Shiraz from strelitzias; Chenin from chrysanthemums?). Granted, given that the largest South African wine corporate has a flagship liqueur made from the fruit of the marula tree, there is a powerful precedent. Or perhaps the WOSA campaign is an ad for the Chelsea Flower Show.

Gluck's larger target, however, is the whole concept of terroir

– that wine should taste of the place in which the grapes were grown – which he variously describes as 'a load of old cobblers', 'complete, utter balderdash from the first syllable of its pretentious and mendacious utterance to its last' and 'a ruse to protect real estate values'.

Stellenbosch wards like the Simonsberg trumpet the unique character of their terroir and then spoil the argument somewhat by making every conceivable style – from sparkling wine to port, by way of Burgundy (Pinot Noir), the Rhône (meaty Shiraz-driven blends) and Bordeaux (Sauvignon Blanc and Cabernet Sauvignon-dominated blends). It's a one-stop world of wine.

Of course, the reason French styles are geographically segregated is legislation, while South African farmers are at liberty to plant anything they think they can sell except dagga (and even then, Grappa distiller Giorgio Dalla Cia would love to include a sprig of *boom* in a bottle, like the Italians do with *ruta*, or rue, calling it *Maria Giovanna*).

For Gluck, terroir is a red herring. For him it is the winemaker who makes the wine, not the soil, aspect or mesoclimate, which are second-order effects at best. The primacy of man over terroir is a contention you must support when you take into account that the magnificent Sauvignon Blancs from Fleur du Cap are made from grapes grown in at least five different appellations (never mind site-specific single vineyards) and wines like the matchless Zonnebloem Laureat 2004 are made in the vineyard of the whole Western Cape.

WOSA marketers must be wondering what they did to deserve the full Gluck treatment. The answer, perhaps, is provided by Gluck's admission that he spent 'hundreds of hours' writing posters for the anti-apartheid movement in his youth and now misses those days, even though 'it seems a terrible thing to say'.

While Gluck is clearly carrying some unresolved issues from a rebellious youth, at least he airs his objections in an entertaining and amusing way. Far better to make a big noise than simmer in silence. A criticism he levels at that other sacred cow of South African wine, *Platter's Wine Guide*, of which he says: 'There is hardly a critical syllable in the whole book. No one speaks his or her mind, as if everything is for the best in the best of all possible worlds and the Cape vineyard is that best place.'

Gluck continues to fire away with both barrels, while others have come to dust: my favourite foreign wine wordsmith, Auberon Waugh, and a South African original, Herman Charles Bosman.

AUBERON WAUGH

The son of the funniest English novelist of the last century continued the brilliant tradition that sometimes spilled over into wine.

I had thought Michael Broadbent's place in the *Guinness Book of Records* for the most politically incorrect description of a wine was inviolate, until I read Auberon Waugh's autobiography, *Will This Do?* (Carroll & Graf, 1998). Auction house Christie's resident wine expert, Broadbent held the record for a description of a magnum of 1947 Château Cantenac Brown as smelling of chocolate and schoolgirl's uniforms. Waugh, wine correspondent for the *Tatler*, went one better when he compared the presentation and appeal of a wine to 'a dead chrysanthemum on the grave of a still-born West Indian baby'.

Hauled before the UK Press Council to answer charges that his description was offensive to West Indians, Waugh had the cheek to claim that the phrase 'West Indian', as applied to wine, 'might suggest a spicy flavour, redolent of guavas and mangoes, excellent in themselves but alien to the true taste of the grape'. The complaint was not upheld.

Waugh's autobiography first appeared in 1991 but was republished in 1998 in a new edition in the United States. Readers' reviews are one reason for buying books on the Internet (the others being a vast selection and cheap prices), whence I ordered *Will This*

Do?. A reader from Washington compares the biography to a poorly edited diary written by a fourth-grader. Another from Connecticut responds: 'The answer to the title's question is a strong "no".'

What the earnest New World reviewers are missing is that Mr Waugh had exceedingly large cheeks, which is where he kept his tongue firmly pressed most of the time. How else could a son of Evelyn Waugh get through life? To say that Waugh's family was dysfunctional is an understatement of the magnitude of describing Sir Laurens van der Post as a bit of a fibber.

In 1943, for example, in order to safeguard his library from any stray flying bombs, Waugh *père* gave instructions that his books be moved to his country house and his son to London:

> 'It would seem from that that I prefer my books to my son. I can argue that firemen rescue children and destroy books, but the truth is that a child is easily replaced, while a book destroyed is utterly lost.'

This attitude was not lost on Waugh *fils*, who ruefully noted: 'The most terrifying aspect of Evelyn Waugh as a parent was that he reserved the right not just to deny affection to his children but to advertise an acute and unqualified dislike of them.'

Waugh senior was a heavy drinker (large quantities of gin mixed with lemon barley water) and had a ferocious temper. In a letter to Nancy Mitford he comments, 'The boy lives for pleasure and is thought a great wit by his contemporaries. I have tried him drunk and I have tried him sober . . . '. Evolution rewards protective adaptations and Waugh junior's sense of irony is accordingly very well developed. Hence his nickname for Waugh senior, 'the august author of my being'.

The ultimate patriarchal put-down is on the cover of the new edition of *Will This Do?* In a lurid gold star there is *Newsweek*'s verdict on the book: 'This is his best book, and as sad and comic as his father's finest work.' Journalist Waugh inherited his father's style of writing in two aspects: overweening snobbery and a mastery of farcical invention. 'Anything pompous or false would be turned on its head, magnified a thousand times and reduced to absurdity', a habit that Waugh II loves indulging.

Waugh's first instinct on being hired to write on wine for the *Tatler* was to adopt a pseudonym. Crispan de St Crispian was chosen on the grounds that it was 'a good Tatlerish name' and wine writing was so important that he wanted the freedom to insult all and sundry in pursuit of the vinous truth. *In vino veritas* and all that.

Of course, his disguise was far from impenetrable and Waugh's identity was soon outed in *Private Eye's* diary section, which is edited by, errh, one A. Waugh. But then, the Brits have always left the responsibilities and conflicts of interest of their wine writers fairly ambiguous, as Jancis Robinson cheerfully admits in her autobiography, *Confessions of a Wine Lover* (her husband is an erstwhile restaurateur and wine importer).

Waugh ran The Spectator Wine Club, where he maintained a loyal band of followers. The Club upholds snobbish standards at all costs. Take Waugh's reaction to the news that research by three French economists concluded that what determines the price of a wine is the label, not the taste. In an experiment involving over 500 bottles of Bordeaux, the panels of experts in various blind tastings determined it was a wine's objective characteristics (primarily the name of the wine and its vintage) which sets its price, rather than it's sensory characteristics. Waugh put the scientists firmly back in their boxes with his claim that 'it is part of the pleasure to know that a wine is famous and very expensive'.

One of Waugh's earliest vinous memories is of the poet Hilaire Belloc, 'an unpleasant old fraud', and Evelyn bottling wine at the family home, Pixton Park, in Somerset. Evelyn would buy a hogshead of Bordeaux, a practice still followed by some oenophiles, and cellar it for a number of years. When mature, the wine would be decanted into individual bottles by candlelight, which considerably slowed the process down, while the adults 'sang idiotic French songs in affected voices'.

One thing about the English upper classes – their houses all have marvellous plummy names. The Waugh brood lived in Combe Florey, a large eighteenth-century house with seven wine cellars. Waugh's master plan was to carry on writing until he has filled up all the cellars with wine and grow simple food on the 35 acres that surround the country pile. At the writing of *Will This Do?* Waugh was halfway there. So retirement was still three and a half cellars off. Alas, it wasn't, as the final cork was pulled in January 2001.

HERMAN CHARLES BOSMAN

The most famous South African short-story writer also had lots to say about wine.

South Africa's greatest short-story writer, Herman Charles Bosman, was born in Kuils River on 3 February 1905 and died in Edenvale Hospital at the age of 46 after an all-night party. He was pretty familiar with the fermented fruit of the vine. As he put it in an autobiographical sketch, *Louis Wassenaar*:

> 'If you write for the press, why can't it be for a wine press? It must be very nice to write for a wine press. Your words will then all come out with thick purple sunshine on them. Your words will be like grapes and your thoughts will be like gold, rich with the splendid intoxication of the summer.'

Although born on the wrong side of the Orange River, Bosman went on to become Johannesburg's greatest literary son. He wrote many short stories and essays about his 'Joh'burg'. Most of his life was lived in the city – in assorted flats and, for a long time, a single room with washbasin in the (now demolished) Sydney Hotel,

where he would write his sublime *Oom Schalk Lourens* stories of
the Bosveld and Groot Marico.

Johannesburg's bars feature prominently in several short stories.
In *Underworld*, the bar is in Fordsburg, while in *Louis Wassenaar*,
the protagonist and a friend meet on Market Street and repair to
the lounge bar of the old Carlton Hotel for a series of brandies.
The bar counter is described as: 'An oval island afloat on a vast
sea of thirst. Was there any time of the day or night when this pub
was not crowded?'

A few drinks later and: 'The edge of the bar counter was the
shining beach of an island that these storm-tossed, shipwrecked
mariners had reached – and that they had been washed up on
the shore a few hours too late.' The old Carlton Hotel no longer
exists – it made way for the new Carlton Hotel, which has now
also closed down.

Bosman's city bars have all but vanished. He would drink Chateau Libertas with the artist Gordon Vorster at the old Langham
Hotel, also gone. Vorster lived a stone's throw away from the Sydney, at the East London Hotel on Loveday Street, and the pair
would often drink in the ladies' bar.

The East London, a marvellous art deco construction next to the
original Brazilian coffee bar, complete with cream conveyor belt,
is still there, but the management now prefers short-term guests.
Accommodation is available at a reasonable R60 per night. A visit
to the ladies' bar of the East London Hotel will show that Bosman
wasn't the only thing to collapse so prematurely.

As Bosman's biographer, Stephen Gray, put it in his introduction to *Bosman's Johannesburg* (Human & Rousseau, 1986): 'like
the city itself in which he collapsed so prematurely', Bosman's work
'remains cubistically scattered, without a hub'.

Alas, wine writing is not what it used to be. Wine columns are
a dying breed and free-lancing a cut-throat business, not least
because several writers submit copy for free, which somewhat
undermines one's argument to the editor for a pay rise. In fact the

best paid berth in the Winelands is the letter to the editor of *WINE* that gets the magnum of Dom Pérignon bubbly prize, worth a couple of grand and tax-free to boot. That option is now closed to me after I used up all my friends as pseudonyms.

NATTERING NABOBS OF NEGATIVISM

The most charismatic South African winemaker accuses local wine hacks of negativity. Has he got a point?

Madame Arcati, the peculiar medium in Noël Coward's comedy *Blithe Spirit*, would be a most appropriate name for an anonymous wine blog. First off, pseudonyms should be feminine, as the traction attained by *Noseweek's* wine pundit as the Widow on www.grape.org. za confirms. Madame Arcati directs events through séances, a most suitable analogue for blind tastings – also often rigged and likewise an attempt to communicate with the dead (in this case, the terroir of vintages past).

Unfortunately, Madame Arcati already exists in the Blogosphere as a scandalous media commentator on madamearcati.blogspot.com. She posts on topics as diverse as photos of Harry Potter in the nude and – staying with the nether regions – which way the testicles of novelist Duncan Fallowell were churning in the New Zealand bath episode of his travelogue *Going as Far as I Can* (Profile, 2008).

It was with a tinge of shame that I read Madame A's blog: 'Delicious row brews between Morrissey and the NME' (*New Musical Express* magazine). The shame was not my adolescent hero worship of Morrissey that refused to clear up when the acne did, but rather that the NME interview is condemned as being 'in the lazy Q'n'A format', a lethargy I indulge in every week via a Q & A column in the *Sunday Times*. It's a most popular format with hacks paid by the word: you only need to write the 'Q' bit, but get paid for the 'A' as well. The victim has to write the 'A' – a quick flick of the editing duster is usually sufficient to lick it into shape.

Kim Maxwell is a past mistress of the format in *WineLand* magazine. She has several victims providing 'A's' to a single 'Q'. Her Q & A 'cults and icons: does South Africa have them yet?' is a good example. The victims – Chris Williams, who makes Meerlust Rubicon, which is already a cult on the banks of the mighty Apies River, and Eben Sadie, an icon among Swartland surfers. The 'A's' Kim got are mixed: '*ja*' from Chris; '*non est*' from Eben, who concludes, 'internal consumer support and positive media backing is lacking'. (And rhyming, too.)

Sadie puts the case much better than the subheadline-writing subeditor:

> 'South Africa is one of the few countries where achieving is a negative. I've never seen such a critical, negative bunch as the South African press. How can consumers change their perceptions if their information is coming from pessimists? Robert Parker changed the way wines are produced in mighty Bordeaux, so don't underestimate the power of the press.'

First, it was not so much Parker who changed Bordeaux, as the curious American phenomenon of buying wine according to a score, an affliction the British (for example) seem much less susceptible to. French and Italian winos are also largely immune, relying on taste buds, rather than eyes, to make decisions. Former Parker associate and lawyer Hannah Agostini does an excellent job of demolishing the pedestal that Parker has long been posing on in her new exposé, *Anatomy of a Myth*, (Scali, 2007) accusing him of being a cut-and-paste specialist with a miraculous ability to rate wines he hasn't even tasted.

Second, any honest member of the local wine-rating circus will confirm there is no local Robert Parker, a person possessed of a palate so influential that it can set consumer trends. And as for the Spiro Agnew charge of South African wine writers being just so many 'nattering nabobs of negativism', perhaps Sadie had the McCarthy (anti-red) campaign of UK authority Tim Atkin in mind, which was indeed taken up by some local wine commentators.

The 'cults and icons' story came out before the Springboks won the World Cup and 'Calamity' Jane MacQuitty unleashed her charge of burnt rubber against South African reds in *The Times*, so that bit of negativism doesn't count. Grape's Widow, sounding awfully like Madame Arcati, but spouting Shakespeare, admonishes me when I raise the odd objection to Platter's platitudes: 'The fault, dear Brutus, is not in our stars, but in ourselves.' So I decided to apply the experimental method of Aristotle to determine in which direction my crystal balls are churning in my *Sunday Times* 'Sidebar' column to see whether I am guilty of undue negativism.

The nine stories published in July and August 2007 (before Sadie's September indictment appeared) deal with – in chronological order – Muratie ☺; Constantia Glen ☺; review of the Swart and Smit terroir book ☹; review of Wishart's malt whisky guide ☺; Bosman Family Vineyards ☺; Sunday Times Food Show ☺ (well, I would, wouldn't I?); Nederburg pre-auction tasting ☺; Woolworth's new Italian wines ☺ and Hendricks Gin ☺. An overwhelming victory for the sunny side of the street. Sadie does have a point, however, for the Nederburg story, excerpted below, makes exactly the same point, but I find a different party guilty:

> 'It was Woody Allen who pointed out that just because you're paranoid, doesn't mean they aren't out to get you. Woody would have made a great South African winemaker and not just because vanilla from oak maturation is a dominant South African wine flavour. After an all-too brief honeymoon following the release of Nelson Mandela in the early nineties, the knives are out for South African wine in a big way.

> 'This was a point made by Dave Hughes, South Africa's most experienced foreign judge (returned from three months

sipping, spitting and swirling in the UK) at a pre-auction tasting for the 33rd Nederburg Auction.

'Hughes divides UK winos into three groups: the punters who love South African wine and buy it; buyers for UK supermarkets who do their level best to deny them and wine writers who slate it. As circumstantial evidence, Hughes credits prejudice against South African wine as a major factor in the rebirth of specialised UK retailers who stock against the status quo and feature such curiosities as South African Chenin Blanc and Pinotage.

'He offered further anecdotal evidence from a trade tasting at Wimbledon: "Flight one consisted of eight South African wines tasted sighted; flight two, eight Aussie wines also tasted sighted, with the Aussie wines scoring 15–20 per cent higher than the South Africans. Flight three was 16 wines (both white and red) tasted blind, with the eight from South Africa the eight best rated."'

Artists of the earth

Extreme winemaking has an appeal to winemakers attempting to squeeze the last millilitre of character from a grape. And it doesn't get more extreme than biodynamic.

It was always a bit of a stretch comparing Beyers Truter, the Prince of Pinotage, to American rock star Prince, as I tried to do in the *Sunday Times*: 'If Beyers Truter was smaller, wore more jewellery, had more hair and spent more time under a sunlamp, he'd be a dead ringer for US rock star Prince.'

The connection was initially made by *Rapport* wine pundit Emile Joubert, who pointed out that everything at the launch of the new all-singing, all-dancing tasting room at Beyerskloof was purple: Pinotage-flavoured ice cream; Pinotage-infused risotto; photos of plump, purple Pinotage grapes on the wall. All it needed was for the Stellenbosch indie rock band in attendance to strike up Prince's colourful anthem, *Purple Rain*.

Which perhaps was the subliminal reason that when the story appeared in print, a photo of Beyers was transposed with one of Michel Laroche – another eponymous winemaker, famous for pioneering screw caps in deeply traditional France and a steely Chablis. Laroche recently purchased L'Avenir Estate on the Simonsberg and is also destined to be famous for Pinotage, if a barrel sample of his Grand Vin Pinotage 2006 is anything to go by.

A one-time photographic model, Michel still cuts a dashing Gallic figure, so perhaps Beyers got the better end of the transposition, especially when Michel was captioned as Beyers Naudé, the well-known cleric and anti-Apartheid activist who died in 2004.

On the subject of Princes, the *Sunday Times* confused another one a few years ago in a story on rum production in Mauritius. The feature was a bit of a fizz, as all the Mauritian Green Island rum is distilled in Durban – the balmy island has a preferential sugar export deal with the EU under the Lomé Convention and it's financially sweeter to export sugar to the EU than to distill it into rum. Something the previous owner of L'Avenir, French-Mauritian Mark Wiehe, can tell you all about.

Which rather did for the rum story, especially as Elizabeth Sejake, the glamorous photographer sent along to snap suitable pics, was a confirmed teetotaler. So when it came to writing up the story, more padding than usual was called for. History is a nice earner for the freelance wine hack, as the word rate for historical background is the same as for thrusting rapier-like tasting insights. So starting with the island's name seemed like a good idea: 'Mauritius was named after Prince Maurits of Orange', which inexplicably appeared in print as 'Prince Charles'.

But the most bizarre case of mistaken identity happed with a story on Meerlust, when the subeditor called to check if Giorgio Dalla Cia was a black grape or green. Neither – he was the winemaker.

Most times, the mistakes go unremarked. However, besmirching national heroes can be assured of an irate letter to the editor. Like the time I interviewed Stellenbosch biodynamic winemaker Johan Reyneke. While the Austrian philosopher Rudolph Steiner is widely regarded as the father of biodynamic winemaking, the ideas go back at least to German polymath Johann Wolfgang von Goethe. Unfortunately, in a feeble attempt at manners, I had referred to Reyneke as 'Johan' in the text and the sub had done a global replace in an attempt to beat my prose into *Sunday Times* brutalist style. The result was repeated references to the famous German philosopher, 'Reyneke Goethe', which elicited a rocket from the director of the Goethe Institute.

Murphy may have a law, but he has no justice, as the credit for biodynamism was pre-Goethe. The English 17th-century botanist Nicolas Culpeper has a stronger paternal claim.

THE FABULOUS, LOST LANGUAGE OF PLANTS

Where do these unusual ideas come from?

Nicholas Culpeper sounds like he could be a character from a J.K. Rowling blockbuster – *Harry Potter and the Biodynamic Bezoar*. An Elizabethan herbalist accused of witchcraft by the medical profession, Culpeper published his masterpiece, *The English Physitian or an Astrologo-Physical Discourse of the Vulgar Herbs of this Nation,* in 1652, the same year that another medical man founded the first European settlement at the Cape.

Culpeper published a helpful homeopathic handbook for the treatment of the everyday ailments of his day, like 'almonds of the ears', 'black and blew spots', 'nepples' and 'purples' (the latter perhaps of interest to Beyers Truter).

Antidotes for 'poyson' were his forte and for which he prescribed a bezoar, or calcified hairball found in the stomachs of cud-chewing animals. His prescriptions read like the potions of the witches of *Macbeth*:

> 'Take of pearls prepared, crab's eyes, red coral, white amber hart's horn, oriental bezoar, of each half an ounce, powder of the black tops of crab's claws, the weight of them all, beat them into powder, which may be made into balls with jelly, and the skins which our vipers have cast off, warily dried and kept for use.'

The kind of remedy our own beetroot-prescribing Minister of Health would no doubt relate to.

Another Nicholas (albeit without an 'h') – Nicolas Joly – is a huge fan and notes: 'Plants have a fabulous language that we have lost. I want to return to the knowledge of plants we had in the Middle Ages – we think they were fools but in fact they were geniuses.' Joly was speaking at a biodynamic winemaking workshop presented to some of the Cape's top vinous alchemists on the eve of the Nederburg Auction in 2005 and it's no coincidence that Joly makes the best Chenin Blanc in France, called La Coulée de Serrant. Scurrilous gossip that Nederburg invited Joly to open their auction because they had confused biodynamism with biodiversity can be safely discounted: the Cape's wine rumour mill insists that corporate parent Distell are considering converting one of their west-coast farms to the biodynamic ethic.

Joly, the Buddha of biodynamism, was the most controversial personality to open the auction since the Minister of Police and Prisons, Jimmy Kruger, did the honours back in 1979. The penny dropped for me during his workshop, when he related how his friend, an Austrian vet, cured a cow by forcing it to eat a live trout. In the biodynamic world, a cow is an inward process and hence linked to water and we all know what fish do in water. It was pure Salvador Dalí, with Joly brandishing an electric field detector in theatrical fashion (like a transistor radio with a shiny aerial), whereas Dalí relied on his waxed moustache tips to pick up electrical emanations from the higher spheres.

The workshop itself was a bit like an episode of the *League of Gentlemen*. But instead of Papa Lazarou exclaiming, 'Oh! this is just a saga now', for Joly, things are either 'absurd' or 'a complete drama'.

Take the concept of winemaker: he finds it 'quite shocking'. 'I hate the phrase,' says Joly. 'You don't make anything. Who's heard of a chickenmaker? A winemaker is a contradiction. On my Japanese business cards, I call myself a "nature assistant".'

Joly sees the 'duty of a wine grower' as communicating the idea that 'working with the earth is an art. We are artists of the earth.' And in the same way that four different artists will produces four different landscapes, so too will four different nature assistants help nature produce four different wines.

Joly takes this idea of helping nature to its logical conclusion by noting that 'life is free and free things have no value. Nature is a gift.

A salad [or a wine for that matter] will not bring you an invoice,' which makes the high prices charged for his Clos de la Coulée de Serrant a contradiction. As was the Institute of Cape Wine Masters charging punters R500 to attend the workshop – especially as the wines served (no Coulée de Serrant, alas) were all donated (thanks to Ken Forrester and Fleur du Cap).

But the biggest contradiction was saved for the auction itself. Directly after he gave his anti-materialistic spiel to assembled wine buyers, prices took off like rockets: R103 per 750ml bottle of dry white wine (up from R54 for the equivalent in 2004) and an incredible R207 for dry red (versus R101 in 2004). So much for the collapse of wine prices that some local pundits had been peddling furiously.

The theme of the workshop was essentially: 'What is an *appellation contrôlée* and how does it work?' and the comment that it's hard to define good wine 'when you've been offered a yeast to give the taste of a Montrachet to a Chenin' raised a few knowing chuckles from assembled 'nature assistants', whose ranks included the industry's young Turks, like Duncan Savage from Cape Point, Adi Badenhorst (at that stage from Rustenberg), Miles Mossop from Tokara and Chris Williams from Meerlust.

Joly bemoaned today's lack of the plant knowledge that was common currency in the Middle Ages for botanists like Culpeper. Joly declared himself to be a holistic thinker: 'The study of the process is important, not the tiny bits of information.' Wine tasting was identified as a process, rather than the recording of sensory descriptors and scoring out of 20 or 100. 'The days of following a great wine critic or a great consultant are over.' If only.

Joly was keen that South African nature assistants follow their own lights, rather than being slavish followers of French fashion: 'I'm interested in trying to find a wine that tastes of South Africa. If [a South African] wine tastes like French wine, what's the point?' His comments were made in the same week that Thomas Do Chi Nam, technical director of Madame May's Château Pichon Lalande, and Tony Moinnereau, an 'award-winning French

sommelier', amongst others, chose 'South Africa's champion Bordeaux blend', as the press release for yet another Michael Fridjhon
competition went (this one sponsored by a French bank and a French
airline, with Fridjhon himself a leading importer of Bordeaux).

It's Joly with bells on if the winning wine is more expensive than
a decent claret like Do Chi Nam's own Château Bernadotte 2001
(available from Fridjhon's Reciprocal Wine Trading), as some of
the South African entries were. This leads to another contradiction
aired by Joly (admittedly from inside a glasshouse, as his Coulée de
Serrant is no price mismark): how come wine is so expensive when
it's ultimately a gift of nature? A contradiction that will blow up in
the faces of top-end producers worse than a well matured stag's
bladder when an icon wine such as Château Le Vieux Télégraphe
sells for less than many local imitations.

In a curious case of gratuitous product placement, MasterCard
conferred local icon status on said Vieux Télégraphe in their South
African TV ad for the best things in life that can be paid for with
plastic, when they featured the wine being served at a romantic
tête-à-tête – an unbeatable marketing opportunity that Vergelegen V's advertising agency would have killed to embrace. And an
answer to that hoary old question as to where South Africa's first
icon wine will come from – France.

Until South African wine stops seeking to impress by imitat-
ing French style, local Bordeaux blends will keep banging their
heads on a Bordeaux ceiling, while the flood of fashionable Rhône
blends are not much better off, with Châteauneuf du Pape's Vieux
Télégraphe sitting on their heads. Local Méthode Cap Classique
producers chasing the champagne chimera are in the same boat
when a bubbly like Tribaut NV, rated four stars by *WINE*, is available for R150 a bottle, including delivery, and Corné Delicatessen
has a handful of famous marques, like Heidsieck Monopole, Pom-
mery, Vranken and Jacquart, priced at well under R200. Although
a timely collapse of the rand/euro exchange rate may bring local
producers some relief.

The twin pillars of local high prices, consumer ignorance and limited importation are fast crumbling as Samsons like David Brice (Wine Cellar), Sam Hackney (Boutique Wines) and Wayne Visser (Great Domaines) expand their activities and market their imports to local wine lovers through a series of restaurant 'wine dinners' that provide unbeatable forums for showcasing wine, with R150,000 worth of orders placed not uncommon. Such events are driving traditional retailers with expensive store rentals to distraction.

M Joly and his campaign for honest wines that taste of the places the grapes were grown is an attractive proposition – sitting through a surreal sideshow a small price to pay for some valuable insights. And besides, it's all great fun.

On the subject of exactly what biodynamism is, Joly drew a musical analogy of a musician, musical instruments and the acoustics of a room. The instrument is terroir, the people involved are musicians and the acoustics are the biodynamics. Conventional farming, with its use of fertiliser ('making a spoilt child out of a vine'), pesticides and herbicides is a 'stupid acoustic. Organic farming is a good acoustic, while biodynamic is an extraordinary acoustic based on the architectural insights of the ancients.'

'All life,' continued Joly, 'is spread between two opposing forces: gravitation and levitation which pulls the plants up like the Greek god Apollo towards the sun.' The trick is to 'tune yourself into the broader reality' and to realise that 'everything is in balance'.

These rhythms of life, which he calls frequencies, are the key. 'We will pay a high price in less than ten years for filling the world with frequencies. There is electrical pollution everywhere.' Joly blames another Nicolas (Tesla, usually spelt Nikola) for the current scourge of electrical pollution which forces him to carry an electric field meter with him on his travels as he can't sleep in an electric field and finds it iniquitous that hotels (Big Cockroach, take note) position lights behind the bed.

'If this was understood,' he claims, 'valium use would decrease by

20 per cent.' (Joly was speaking before valium was exposed as nothing more than an expensive placebo.) Mobile phones, of course, are
'a complete drama' and when he flies, he always requests a seat in the
middle of the plane where electrical pollution is minimum and seats
his wife at the window.

On the subject of cork taint, Joly offered a novel explanation and a
solution:

> 'Cork is a complete drama. Some large companies overpaid
> for their cork forests and so insisted on an increased yield.
> The result was a decrease in quality. All the rest is blah, blah,
> blah. I have great respect for people choosing screw caps,
> but I'm still too conservative to change (it's all in my mind, I
> know). Before I use a cork, I insist that suppliers sign a letter
> of undertaking to replace all corked bottles, at their expense.
> If they have confidence in their product, they will sign.'

To criticise Joly for the arcana of his craft – burying cow horns filled
with manure and hanging a stag's bladder stuffed with yarrow in a
tree – besides being boring, is to miss the point. His aim is to highlight the contradictions in our thoroughly modern world of techno-
logically driven wine.

Joly, a former merchant banker for Morgan Guaranty in New York,
is, as UK wine pundit Andrew Jefford noted on a trip to Paarl as a
Toasty judge, 'the best advertisement for biodynamic winemaking',
since he looks several decades younger than his chronological age,
with vim and vigour aplenty.

Conventional wisdom, in the shape of *Harpers* magazine, holds
that biodynamic farming has its roots (no pun intended) in lectures delivered in 1924 by the Austrian philosopher-scientist Rudolf
Steiner, whose 'life mission was to bridge the gap between the
material and spiritual worlds through the philosophical method'.
To this end he established Waldorf schools and, shortly before his
death, turned his attention to agriculture in a series of lectures

entitled 'Spiritual Foundations for the Renewal of Agriculture'.

Steiner's big idea was a holistic one of considering a farm as a living system in the context of a wider pattern of cosmic rhythms. For example, soil is not regarded as dirt, but rather a living organism in its own right, hence the antipathy biodynamists have towards pesticides. As Joly notes: 'These people are drug dealers. They sell you pesticides which kill your soil and then chemical fertilisers to make plants grow. Farmers soon become addicts, dependent on their chemical fix.'

Just as many results in modern mathematics are rediscoveries of work done by Russians in previous generations but never published in the West, so too are most of the radical and new theories of Steiner simply restatements of the common knowledge from a previous age. Culpeper noted in an advertisement for his book: 'Herein is also shewed . . . what Planet governeth every Herb or Tree that groweth in England and the Time of gathering all Herbs, both Vulgarly and Astrologically.' This four centuries before Steiner's commentary on cosmic rhythms and farming according to lunar cycles.

Home for Joly is a medieval monastery (think *The Name of the Rose* – the occupant a Gallic rather than Gaelic Sean Connery and with more hair), built in a hollow (the *coulée* of his famous brand) by Cistercian monks in the 12th century. He prefers to live next to his terroir at the bottom of the valley so he can be close to the earth forces and his vines, which are tangibly linked to the earth, while his mother lives 'in a permanent nirvana' at the top of the hill.

He literally lives according to his principles and it's all a little bit Amish. Tractors (described as 'boom-boom processes') have been replaced by four horses (although only one does any work, the other three 'belong to the landscape'), since Joly likes 'the impulsion provided by animals' and the electricity is switched off at night, as the ghost of electricity is the big bogeyman of biodynamism.

Strilli Oppenheimer, who has been managing her 20-hectare Brenthurst garden in biodynamic fashion for 30 years, agrees with

Joly's fatwa on cellphones and holds them responsible for the large decrease in insect types and numbers in her Parktown garden. One unusual feature she brings to the biodynamic debate is the requirement that the 50 gardening staff join her and head gardener Dawid Klopper in 40 minutes of t'ai chi twice a week.

According to Joly, the planets and the zodiac 'are the most exciting' part of biodynamic winemaking and winemakers can use them to tune in to various cosmic forces. Then there are the specific remedies, like flower heads of yarrow or cow manure fermented in a cow's horn and buried in the soil, which Joly calls 'telephone numbers to connect to a specific process'. Manure is a fascinating subject for Joly. From his Cuban cigars made from tobacco grown by Alejandro Robaina, who only uses horse manure, to the best producer of sake in Japan (who uses duck guano), Joly sees manure as containing a vegetal impregnation of the metabolism of an animal.

In the Joly cellar, intervention – like electricity – is minimal. He uses no yeasts and fermentations take place with no temperature control, nor are the lees removed. Wines are left to age in barrels with their egg-like shapes replicating the life force. The shape of the barrel should reflect the latitude of the winery, which explains why those of Burgundy and Bordeaux differ and is something for South African producers at far lower latitudes than their French colleagues to consider. To explain just how important barrels are, Joly notes that any dog would far rather sleep in an empty barrel than a kennel because of its life-giving shape. 'It's important to rediscover the sense of shapes', he maintains.

Interestingly, Marc Kent, 'nature assistant' and artist of the earth at Boekenhoutskloof, has recently acquired an egg-shaped maturation vessel. Shortly after the egg arrived, Marc won the Diners Club Winemaker of the Year Award for his Syrah. Coincidence?

Joly's recent research has focused on using clay amphorae to store wine as was the custom of the ancient Greeks and Etruscans. While clay has various life-affirming properties ('clay can cure; it is strongly linked to the sun,' explains Joly), it is their shape that is the clincher – inverted medieval cathedrals in miniature and, as such, they channel the Dionysus force. 'It's all a question of frequencies,' he continues. 'I know a man who put Chartres Cathedral inside a small box by replicating frequencies.'

With biodynamic wines scarcer in South Africa than unicorn horns, a blend of Shiraz and Merlot called the Philosopher's Stone made by Johnny Nel at his Camberley Vineyards on the top of Hellshoogte, should qualify as an honorary biodynamic wine. After all, J.K. Rowling did write a book about that one. Another exponent is Johan Reyneke, who consults to Boekenhoutskloof.

JOHAN REYNEKE

A chat with the local hero of biodynamic winemaking.

Walking in the vineyards at Reyneke Wines, just off the Polkadraai Road in Stellenbosch, is a bit like ambling on a travelator at O.R. Tambo Airport – every step has a small spring in it. Percussive proof that the biodynamic farming practices adopted by owner Johan Reyneke produce soils that are markedly different from those farmed using conventional methods.

Yet the wines from Reyneke are so low profile, they're essentially invisible. Although chances are you've drunk wine made from his fruit, as he sells his biodynamic grapes to high-profile producers like De Toren, Tokara and Boschendal. But all that might be about to change as Johan embarks on a process of 'adding values ourselves. We produce 2,000 cases of wine in a converted cowshed, but grow enough grapes for 25,000.'

A self-declared farmer as opposed to marketer, Johan contacted the savviest distributor in the business in the shape of Tim Rands, MD of Vinimark, 'to find out how to make our wines more available'. Tim was so impressed, he invested the suitably biodynamic sum of a new home for Johan, wife and baby daughter. 'I was sick and tired of living in a one-room cottage,' says Reyneke.

Johan is the most unassuming winemaker in an industry bristling with prima donnas and I-specialists. 'If I'm lucky, I'll be on this farm for eighty years,' he muses. 'And these guys were here one-and-a-half million years ago,' he adds, holding a hand axe that stars on his wine label. 'I plan to leave it at least as good as I found it.' Which is well on track, thanks to his embrace of biodynamism.

Johan explains that the easiest way to understand biodynamic methods is in comparison to competing systems like conventional farming, which is essentially cost-driven and biological, or organic farming, which adopts a more sustainable approach.

Take weeds, for example. For biodynamists, a farm is a book and weeds are letters on a page. 'Instead of fighting them, we should read them as symptoms of an underlying problem,' explains Johan. He enumerates three contentious aspects:

A farm is viewed holistically as a nurturing entity and the objective is to maximise life on it: from the microbial content of the soil to the plants, insects and birds. A stable ecosystem with sufficient biological diversity is a prerequisite. The second aspect consists of biodynamic treatments which are applied to the soil (with cow dung matured in a horn buried in winter and exhumed in summer, perhaps the most unusual). Then comes the role of the moon and the stars, which govern the timing of the various farming practices applied.

Q: Why did you decide to go biodynamic?

A: I was doing a postgraduate degree in environmental ethics and wanted to farm and make wine in an environmentally friendly way. At that stage there was a bit of a backlash about organic wines being eco-friendly, but not living up to the quality of their conventional counterparts. One evening, I was dining with our Scandinavian agent in Copenhagen and we tasted a whole range of conventional, organic and biodynamic wines blind. One in particular just got better and better throughout the evening, and (at three in the morning) it turned out to be a bottle of Nicolas Joly's Coulée de Serrant.

*As a parting present, I was given Joly's book and, though it was fas-
cinating, I found it a bit too esoteric at first. Back in South Africa I
went to see Jeanne Malherbe who has been farming biodynamically in
Wellington since 1969. She offered a lot of practical advice and introduced me to the writings of Peter Proctor and Alex Podolinsky. They
are biodynamic specialists from New Zealand and Australia and also
take a more practical approach. I think there are also important differences in terms of southern and northern hemisphere conditions. Our
sun is a lot harsher and we also have a much lower organic content
in our soils.*

Q: How long have you been at it?

*A: We started off as a commercial farm in 1988, then moved to organ-
ics in 1997 and finally started implementing biodynamic principles in
2000. We did it in various stages and only converted our last vineyards
in 2004. This is something I would recommend to all newcomers, as it is
a completely different way of understanding your relationship to nature
as a whole.*

Q: Did you notice a difference?

*A: Most definitely. The first big difference is the soil. In our dry sum-
mers, if you try to put your hands into the soil of one of our vineyards
that has only recently been converted, it is not possible because the
soil is so hard and compact. If you try to do so in a vineyard which
has been farmed in this way for some time, your hand will go in past
your wrist.*

*The second difference is the marked increase in numbers and diversity of
small animals, birds and insects. There are insects and birds on our farm
that I've never seen before. The vines have also lost some of their vigour,
the grapes are smaller and the bunches are less compact. A lot of difficult
weeds have disappeared two to three seasons after we stopped with the*

herbicides and we have more grasses and wild vetches now. We constantly try and add beneficial plants and herbs to this process. Mealybug has almost completely disappeared. I believe it is because we planted clover, which is their natural habitat.

In general, I'll say that the vines are in a better balance within themselves as well as with their natural environment. There is also quite a big difference in the cellar. We only do natural wild-yeast fermentations and have had no problems in this regard. (I was told that the fungicides used for downy and powdery mildew weakens the natural yeast on the grape and that this is why one so often gets stuck fermentations when you do a wild-yeast fermentation with conventionally grown grapes.) We add no enzymes, do no protein stabilisations or magic of any kind. Only very light filtrations where necessary.

Q: Is there any downside?

A: I think the biggest downside is that people reject biodynamics because they either feel threatened by it, or see it as a very weird system of thought. With regard to the first, this should definitely not be the case. As recently as this morning, I had a long discussion with my (conventional) neighbour to discuss the sowing of our cover crops. We were adjusting implements and looking at the moisture content of the soil and so on. I guess what I'm trying to say is that good farming practice will always carry more weight than any particular system: one should never try to force reality to cope with your ideology. With regard to the 'weirdness' of biodynamics, I think both the proponents of biodynamics as well as those who ridicule it should relax somewhat. I think we should agree that biodynamics is a completely different way of looking at things and if one is not able to make this paradigm switch (ie those relatively new to biodynamics or not very philosophically inclined), you will try to understand biodynamics from the traditional perspective where it certainly does not make sense and may, indeed, seem very strange.

I personally advocate a softer and a harder approach with which one can explain biodynamic actions. For example, if one takes the use of the preparation 500 (cow dung stuffed into a horn and buried in the vineyard), the soft explanation would rather be done at the level of matter. In this context it is good to bury the manure in a cow horn (as opposed to a Tupperware container) due to its naturally higher level of bacteria, which in turn act as a catalyst to boost the production of microorganisms. When this preparation is stirred vigorously in the way that is advised, it boosts the vitality and numbers of microorganisms with all the oxygen that now comes into the mixture.

The harder explanation would be done at the level of energy. Here the cow horn is seen as a very special receptacle of energy, and the vortex in which the preparation is stirred is seen as the way in which nature very often manifests itself through energy (ie water running from a bath, a breaking wave, a tornado, petal formation on a flower or whatever). Being a relative newcomer to biodynamics, I prefer to use both the softer and the harder explanation to understand it.

A possible analogy between the debate on conventional versus biodynamic paradigm could be the scientific paradigm. Do we explain our reality with the help of Newton or Einstein? To me it is not so important to analyse and explain why things actually work, but rather to know that they do work. In the case of biodynamics, proof fortunately exists. Geisenheim University has been running concurrent trials with conventional, organic and biodynamic produce for many years now and the results are freely available.

Q: What has been the biggest benefit?

A: Marketing – no, just kidding! I'd say being closer to nature in both a physical and spiritual way. And also having a green spring with insects, birds and flowers amongst the vines, for sure.

ART OR CRAFT?

After buying a farm on the Paardeberg, I decide to become an artist.

While Johan Reyneke is undoubtedly an artist of the earth, is he really on the same wavelength as David Hockney? Is the wine cellar the new art studio? While icon wines from rare vintages may attract silly money on auction, just like Dylan Lewis's big-cat sculptures did at Christie's in 2007, no art critic would dare to score William Kentridge 17 out of 20 or award him a rating out of 100 in the same way that wines are assessed. Conversely, while many a parent may claim their child can paint better than Pablo Picasso, Jean-Michel Basquiat or Tracey Emin, few would claim their offspring could produce an Yquem.

That said, wine and art do have a lot in common. There is similar confusion over exactly what makes fine art – Damien Hirst's diamond-encrusted skull, *For the Love of God*, sold recently for $100 million, being a good example.

Over in the South African spittoon, the pointy-tongued pundits of the Platter guide rated the Woolworth's selection of Duncan Savage's Cape Point 2007 Sauvignon Blanc a full house of five stars; at the same time, the pundits of *WINE* magazine in Pinelands scored the same wine a lowly one star.

And the goalposts of both wine and art change continually. Where have all those acidic Premier Grand Crus of the 70s and 80s gone, or the magnums of Blanc de Noir? The same way as the voluptuous Venuses of Rubens, squeezed out of the beauty stakes by Twiggy, Kate Moss and a new aesthetic heroin-chic model.

But can wine ever be art? Wine is, above all, a natural process. As Paul Draper, philosopher and winemaker at Ridge Vineyards in California, puts it: 'What is fine wine all about? Let's start from the point that making a wine is a natural process.' Just like the works of Andy Goldsworthy, the land artist who sculpted a snake out of sand at Donald Hess's art gallery at the Glen Carlou winery in 2008 after filming the shadows cast by leaves in a babbling brook.

Draper claims: 'For me, it's a bond of trust with the soil, the place, the land itself.' This sounds a lot like a statement from artist Strijdom van der Merwe, whose red flags on the barren hillside above the Rooiberg Winery do so much to chirp up the start of the Robertson Wine Route. As do those waving yellow hands on the R44 (which I thought were an ad for Simba Nik Naks) in the vineyard of Oude Libertas in Stellenbosch.

Then there is the temporal nature of wine. Even the greatest vintages eventually turn to vinegar. Destroyed just like the Bloubergstrand sculptures of Van der Merwe when the tide comes in or Leonardo's *Last Supper*, which needs to be continually refreshed or it will simply fade away (and where would Dan Brown and his conspiracy theories be then?).

In a conversation with Andrew Jefford, the UK's best wine writer by a country mile, in *Questions of Taste: the Philosophy of Wine* (edited by Barry Smith, Signal, 2007), Draper agrees with Jefford's assertion: 'Greatness in wine comes primarily from its place of origin, but requires the will and experience of the wine grower to be able to express its greatness. Wine is not, therefore, an artistic creation like a piece of music or a sculpture.' Jefford is rolling out the old terroir hobby horse and taking it for a ride.

Draper agrees: 'Wine is not a created work. What we do is more akin to what a performer does with a piece of music.' But then, as Marcel Duchamp proved a century ago with his ready-mades (including a urinal he cheekily titled 'Fountain'), while some winemakers (or winegrowers as Draper prefers to be known, or 'nature assistants' as Joly puts it) and some wine writers may declare that wine is not art, artists are quite at liberty to call anything they like art – including the fermented fruit of the vine.

So when the invitation to exhibit at the Sixth Sense art exhibition at Monte Casino fizzed through the Internet and into my inbox, my ears pricked up. The exhibition is held in conjunction with the annual conference of the PR Institute of Southern Africa

(PRISA), which for 2008 had as its theme 'Communication – the Sixth Sense'. In addition to the aforesaid exhibition, the invitation promised 'an environmental ballet created on this theme' plus 'a mega-fashion show in which garments will depict the six senses'.

The point of departure for the exhibition, ballet and fashion show was the medieval tapestry *La Dame à la Licorne*, the maiden and the unicorn, which has the six senses as leitmotif and is to be seen at the Cluny Museum in Paris. One of the masterpieces of medieval art, it would not look out of place in the faux-medieval piazzas and palaces of Monte Casino.

The six senses are the traditional five: touch, taste, smell, hearing and sight plus a further sense 'which arises from the interaction between stimuli from the outer world and the inherent knowledge of the inner world'. Wine obviously titillates the five traditional senses, while terroir makes a strong case for informing a sixth. As has been proved many times in experiments involving CAT scans and the like, the brain's enjoyment of wine is not totally derived from sensory input. Prior knowledge – knowing a wine is expensive, for example – improves the tasting experience no end.

Having bought Lemoenfontein, a modest wine farm on the Paardeberg, in 2007, I decided to make the most traditional wine I could from ancient bush-vine Pinotage grapes growing on the farm's steep slopes. The connection between the wine and the medieval tapestry is compelling. A maiden vintage (*la dame*) from a mountain famous for quaggas (the Boere version of the mythical unicorn and likewise extinct). The grapes were harvested on St Valentine's day, which could explain the dreamy lovelorn expression of the lady depicted in the tapestry.

The wine was made together with three friends (Stellenbosch winemakers Donovan Rall and Johan Kruger in the Nabygelegen cellar of James McKenzie) in the Bovlei valley above Wellington, and the cooperative nature of the winemaking process mimics the teams of weavers responsible for the tapestry. Both are handmade with no artificial technology used at all – the wine was fermented using wild yeasts and matured in third-fill French oak barrels, confirming the French connection.

The Sixth Sense exhibition curator, Mixael de Kock, unwittingly supplies the final thread. His CV lists '380 major national exhibitions between 1976 and 1992 – the majority of these under the label of Stellenbosch Farmers' Wineries' wines'. It's hard to imagine, therefore, an artwork more completely in accordance with the exhibition brief than a barrel of Lemoenfontein Pinotage, which we have decided to call The Six Ps. The first five, arranged alphabetically, are Paardeberg, Pendock (the artist), Perold (the pioneer who produced Pinotage by crossing Cinsault with Pinot Noir), Pinotage and PRISA. The final P is a pee, the ultimate end-state of the work once it has passed through the body.

Of course sale of the work to a collector (or failing that, a drinker) might be a tricky issue, as the exhibition is unlikely to have a liquor licence. But then, this barrel is a work of art and any resemblance to a barrel of wine is purely coincidental.

Artists of the gallery - a cultural symbiosis

Exploring the connection between art and wine from the studio.

Winemaker Tom Riley is the international face of Penfolds, the South Australia wine behemoth. In adspeak:

> 'Son of a psychiatrist and an artist, Tom was perhaps pre-destined to become a winemaker – inheriting both genuine creativity and a keen, inquiring mind . . . An award-winning artist in his spare time, Tom sometimes feels that the creative lines are blurred – just as he paints with colour, he creates masterpieces of flavours as a winemaker.'

(Advertisement for Penfolds in *The Spectator*)

Which simultaneously resolves the nature versus nurture debate and demotes Tom's art to a commercial context from which it will battle to escape.

Posing in an ad in *The Spectator* alongside a moody painting and a bottle of Bin 28 in gothic black, Tom is the spitting image of Donovan, that psychedelic Glaswegian hippie from the swinging sixties whom a hopelessly optimistic advertising industry proposed as a UK Dylan. While some artists of my acquaintance are heroic drinkers – like C.J. Morkel, who shatters the silence of Calitzdorp as he blasts oil paintings of pornographic veggies with his .44 magnum, high on gin and talent – many wine estates return the favour with their art.

The Lourensford property of retail tycoon Christo Wiese is now home to a branch of the Bell-Roberts Gallery, while Dick Enthoven's Spier spread in Stellenbosch (motto: 'Discovering the

art in wine since 1692') plays host to a new biennial contemporary art competition that showcases the talents of a hundred young
South African artists from across the land. This marriage of fine art
and fine wine is a good example of cultural symbiosis.

Even Uitkyk, that Mrs Haversham of the Winelands, discovered
some eighteenth-century murals on the walls and restored them to
their somber glory. The all-singing, all-dancing tasting room was
laid out by a geomancer with a central water-filled gutter, providing
serious feng shui. During his infamous design demolition derby, Sir
Terence Conran exclaimed, 'An al fresco urinal. How jolly!'

JEFF KOONS

America's most famous artist has a beautiful South African connection.

Was it a case of synchronicity that the electrons bearing the news that
French authorities are allowing the use of oak chips to flavour their
wines arrived shortly after lunch with Jeff Koons? Koons, arguably
the most famous living artist, made a name for himself in the 80s
with stainless-steel sculptures of giant inflatable rabbits and vacuum
cleaners standing silently in glass vitrines.

One of the images Koons presented at a lecture at Wits University was a gaily painted bouquet of daisies carved in wood and presented as such. Or was it perhaps, as Koons said, 'a bunch of fifty
assholes'? Which is probably what some French winemakers think
of the apparatchiks of the CNAOC (France's national *appellation
d'origine contrôlée* confederation), which made the decision to permit oak shavings, spinning cones and listing grape cultivars on wines
above the *vin de pays* level.

Koons had agreed to talk at Wits, as that's where his wife, Justine,
studied fine art. I'd just bought a digital dictaphone from Kalahari.
net and thought the Koonival was the perfect occasion to try it out.
The dictaphone captured verbatim Professor Penny 'Pinky-Pink'
Siopis' gushing welcome introduction. But the great man's address

ARTISTS OF THE GALLERY - A CULTURAL SYMBIOSIS

was unintelligible. Having had recent well-documented copyright problems, this technology-savvy artist was taking no chances, jamming all recordings.

After his standing room-only performance, Penny and her motley crew of Fine Art Profs and hangers-on descended on De Luxe restaurant in Milpark, where another Wits fine art graduate, Andrea Burgner, had prepared bowls of cucumber gazpacho and platters of spicy Thai fishcakes and salad.

South Africa is starting to feature in the Koons iconography. His latest paintings use Cape Town as backdrop for giant cartoon figures – Popeye, Olive Oil and the Incredible Hulk. But the highlight of the Koons talk were images from a 1986 exhibition, 'Luxury and Degradation', held at the International with Monument gallery in New York's Lower East Side.

Koons's idea was brilliant in its simplicity. Starting in one of the poorest neighbourhoods of New York, he took a subway to Grand Central, slap bang in the rich core of the Big Apple. Along the way, he recorded advertisements for alcohol presented to commuters.

In neighbourhoods where the income was less than $10,000 p.a. the text was Spanish; the product advertised Bacardi rum in a casino setting featuring a pair of dice. The message: life is a gamble and alcohol is your bet.

Moving up to $25,000 p.a., skyscrapers of Dewars whisky bottles mimicked the Manhattan skyline, while at $40,000 it was a wild-west steam train, faithfully transformed into stainless steel, with a bottle of Jim Beam under the smokestack and another in the guard's van.

Arrival at Grand Central was represented by the travel bar: a faithful reproduction (again in stainless steel) of a 1950s Tiffany-style picnic basket for alcoholics: cocktail shaker, glasses, decanter with liquor sealed inside and unobtainable without destroying the work. A potent metaphor for the charms of advertising.

Koons remarked that one of the attractions of his fetishistic vacuum cleaners was the wet/dry capability, which he likened to

Sartre's being/nothingness. This appropriation of 'ready-mades' predictably splits the art world into appalled purists and fans. Probably in the same proportions as the French addition of wood shavings will divide anoraks (or cagoules, as they call them over there).

Hopefully, the price of first growths will fall, as wood chips are cheaper than barrels in the same way that a 'Rolex' bought on a Fifth Avenue sidewalk is much cheaper than one from Tiffany & Co.

Of course, a wood chip Bordeaux is not a counterfeit wine, just a manufactured one (and for Koonsians, a kitsch wine). US art critic Clement Greenberg, in his essay *Avant-Garde and Kitsch*, describes kitsch as 'the debased and academicised simulacra of genuine culture' and while the avant-garde 'imitates the processes of art, kitsch imitates the effect'.

Fine wine is no less a cultural artefact than a Koons bunny sculpture or Popeye painting, and Greenberg's kitsch argument applies to wine. In the same way that Koons appropriates the forms and techniques of classical art to manufacture works that required absolutely no effort on the part of the viewer to understand them, so too is wood chip Bordeaux a simulacrum of classic claret – one that wine show judges are sure to appreciate.

Fine art is becoming incredibly fashionable in the Winelands and the gallery with maximum international cred is the Hess Collection on Glen Carlou estate in Paarl.

DONALD 'IL MAGNIFICO' HESS

The owner of one of the most important collections of contemporary art decides to build a gallery on his Paarl wine estate.

Synchronicity – meaningful coincidence – was one of the big ideas of Swiss psychologist Carl Jung, and chance is a vineyard worker that has at least as much effect on wine quality as the deterministic actions of the most diligent winemaker. So it's quite appropriate that the first artwork you see in the new gallery inside the Glen

Carlou tasting room is by Scottish artist Andy Goldsworthy, whose métier is creating art by chance.

Goldsworthy's work consists of mini-moraines of soil and dirt on paper left by melting snowballs. The shapes formed by the retreating ice are strangely organic in form and their muted russets and reds echo views of the distant Drakenstein Mountains from the giant windows of the thatched boma-style tasting room above a fynbos Zen garden. That they should be here, now, is also the outcome of a random process, the role of some cosmic dice, for Swiss property magnate, hotelier and one-time brewer Donald Hess nearly didn't buy the farm.

Seeking to diversify his assets of 'one small brewery, a hotel in Tangiers and a tiny winery in the French part of Switzerland', bequeathed by his dad, Hector, Donald flew to Calistoga, California, to shop for a mineral-water spring. The United States was a natural choice for diversification, as both his mother and first wife were American. A lover of powerful wines, he ended up with a wine farm in the Napa Valley, which quickly became a financial success and, more importantly, a passion. Today, the Napa operation farms 1,000 hectares and produces over seven million bottles of wine.

With an eye open for a bargain, Hess visited the South African Winelands in 1993, which were then well and truly in an apartheid laager, excluded from international innovation for a generation by politics and battling sanctions and export boycotts.

'I visited 13 or 14 wineries, but turned up no world-class wines,' says Hess. 'A friend of mine, a British wine writer, was coming to South Africa and asked for my tasting notes. After his trip he sent me a couple of bottles. "You missed two wineries – Thelema and Glen Carlou." I tasted the Glen Carlou and agreed it was first rate. A call to owner Walter Finlayson, a trip to Paarl and the deal was done in 48 hours.'

A winery in South Australia (Peter Lehmann) and establishing the highest vineyards in the world (at over 3000 m), in north-east Argentina at Bodega Colomé, were next on the agenda. Colomé was the oldest winery in Argentina, dating back to 1831, with 150-year-old Malbec vines that produce wines of extraordinary concentration and complexity.

After travelling the world for 45 years, Donald has now settled down to the travel rhythms of a migratory bird: six months in a former monastery outside Berne and six months in Argentina at Colomé, 'the youngest of my children that needs my support the most'.

Perhaps the most noteworthy aspect of the Hess wine empire is the integration of fine art into his business – the name 'Collection' for his wine brand is apt. Hess is a firm believer in contemporary art for the people ('collectors who keep their art in a bank vault are despicable') and notes that 'people interested in fine wine are often also interested in art', so to locate an art gallery inside a tasting room makes complete sense.

Reflecting on the similarities between fine wine and fine art, Hess notes:

> 'Both are life-enhancing. Both are beautiful. They've always been associated – the Romans did it and the French too – look at Château Mouton Rothschild and their labels. Our achievement is to have established the first contemporary art gallery inside a winery (at Mount Veeder in the Napa Valley).'

Hess calls himself 'a collector' and admits the key to being successful is to be 'a dictator'. He follows a couple of rules:

> 'I try not to be influenced by fashion. I buy art from living artists who must be professional and dedicated. My test is: "Would I defend this art on American TV?" My acquisitions are my children – and I have a thousand of them. If you ask me for a favourite, it's like asking a mother to choose a favourite child. Maybe the one who is sick, the one who has the most problems.'

Would he feel confident defending an artwork? 'Yes. The work belongs to me, but not the idea.'

With the fine-art market on a roll and each auction setting new price records, Hess notes: 'Good art has nothing to do with big sums of money. The secret is to trust yourself. Museums look for high prices to validate their decisions, which leads to a vicious upward spiral of prices. It's absolutely stupid.' That said, his art addiction has saved a fortune on therapy: 'One of my first purchases was by Alfred Jensen. He was into American Indian culture and I bought a work consisting of lots of coloured squares. After a hard day, I'd spend some time looking at it – it saved me going to a psychiatrist. My paintings are my therapy.'

And how does he choose them? 'When I see an artwork, I look at it, then go home and sleep. If I can sleep, it's not for me. It has to touch my soul. If I wake up several times during the night thinking about it, I buy it.'

The new gallery is divided into two spaces: a large central core that Hess would like to dedicate to African and South African art and an oblong foyer for international works, which will be rotated every year. Glen Carlou's winemaker and general manager, David Finlayson, said getting the artworks installed was 'a nightmare'. The art came from Luxembourg and the insurance company insisted on an armed escort from Johannesburg airport at a cost of US$9,000.

Two days before the opening, curator Myrtha Steiner was almost in tears, as the gallery was so humid that the delicate Goldsworthys were absorbing water and threatening to morph. So it was out with the heaters and a campaign of serious climate control. The gallery itself is hermetically separated from the winery as the climatic conditions conducive to wine maturation are anathema to artworks.

The Glen Carlou gallery is Hess's second in a winery. The first was a conversion of his hundred-year-old, three-storey, limestone Napa winery into a stunning gallery with crisp white walls and ceilings, bleached oak floors and panoramic views of the volcanic slopes of Mount Veeder.

The main area of the Glen Carlou space features an exhibition of works by Durban artist and one-time Professor of Colour at the Royal Academy in London Deryck Healey, who died in 2004. This fulfils a promise Hess made to the artist that he would be the first to show in the new gallery. A friend for over 30 years, Hess describes Healey as 'quite eclectic. He doesn't have a style. He makes sculptures and paintings from found objects which he calls "my dumb friends". I love his paintings and towards the end (he had cancer) he ended up painting on his knees. I bought three – but they got lost somewhere.'

Hess likes to develop a personal relationship with the artists he collects and to talk to them (with the exception of Frank Stella, who was notoriously mute on the subject of his work). The Hess Collection features such superstars as the German neo-expressionist Georg Baselitz, whom Hess describes as 'fascinating, but shy to the point of rudeness. If you don't know him, you'd think him arrogant.'

On Francis Bacon, of the screaming popes and butcher-shop carcasses, Hess says:

> 'An extraordinary man. He was an unhappy homosexual and through that, started to drink. If you knew his background, you'd think him dumb and brutal. But he was the opposite – very well read, very accurate and very interesting when he wasn't smashed. He was very opinionated and could also be very rude. He loved my first wife, Joanna, and we'd often meet at the Connaught Bar in the art heart of London and he'd say, "Joanna, come and sit right next to me."'

Gilbert and George – two men who have pursued a joint career as a single artist – are also on the list. 'When you go to their studio in Spitalfields, they play good theatre,' says Hess. 'They offer you a cup of tea and there's this whole staged Victorian environment. Of course, they make their art in another place. I've got about 10 pieces – but their excrement works are too much for me.' One of Hess's Gilbert and Georges is called *Flight* and portrays a flock of latter-day Icaruses who soar above two figures standing on the ground, holding wine glasses. The heads of the flying people lie scattered around the pair, a salutary statement about the dangers of drinking and flying, perhaps.

And would he ever commission an artwork? 'No. I'm not for the medieval system where artists weren't free.' And commissioning special works for his wineries? 'I'd hope the artist would have the guts to tell me he's an artist, not an interior decorator.'

Speaking of which, Toni Tollman was an interior designer in Manhattan before taking on her family's Red Carnation portfolio of boutique hotels in Europe. She was also responsible for the interiors of the new Cape Dutch manor house on the Bouchard Finlayson property outside Hermanus, which she stuffed full of contemporary art, advised by Cape Town dealer Michael Stevenson. Sister Vicki manages the family wine business.

BACCHUS WEARS BLAHNIK: VICKI TOLLMAN

Mr Hess is not the only estate owner with an art addiction.

Vicki Tollman is about as far away from the wine anorak stereotype as you could imagine. So what is she doing sipping Chardonnay from almost unbreakable Juliet Cullinan Mikasa stemware, while discussing the merits of Abrie Bruwer's Botrytis-influenced Méthode Ancienne versus Danie de Wet's Bateleur?

> 'My father, Stanley, is a classic bon vivant and, as kids, we were brought up with wine. When he invested in Bouchard Finlayson in the Hemel en Aarde valley six years ago (he said, "got involved"), I enrolled in a crash course at L'Université du Vin in Morges, Provence. We tasted wine in a 12th-century chapel – I thought I'd died and gone to heaven. It ignited a passion. Our winemaker, Peter Finlayson, has been a wonderful teacher and now wine has become a passion.'

One she indulges from a distance, as Geneva is now home, where she works in the marketing activities of the family Red Carnation Collection hotel group, with seven properties in the UK, and one in Geneva and Palm Beach. Vicki gets down to South Africa between four and six times a year:

> 'We also have the Twelve Apostles Hotel and Spa at Oude-kraal, on the coast between Camps Bay and Llandudno, as well as Bushman's Kloof in the Cederberg. I am involved in the marketing for all our properties and two years ago I brought my three daughters out with me and we even made some wine: we stomped pinot grapes in a big tank and Peter made a wine he called 'twinkle toes'. My daughter did a project on Sauvignon Blanc for a school in Geneva – she would phone Peter and ask for advice on fermentation, although they're all too young to be drinking too much of it!'

Vicki was schooled in Johannesburg at Redhill (she was in the same class as Donny Gordon's son, Graham). The family left South Africa in the 70s and Vicki admits Johannesburg has changed so much since she left, 'it's now a city I know without knowing. I wanted to show my daughters our family home in Empire Place. It's changed a lot to how I remembered it as a child, but the material on the ceiling is still the same. It was very moving going back'. So why did she? So her girls could get a taste of her childhood and relate to the memories and stories she often tells them of the past.

> 'After apartheid, my dad wanted to invest in land in South Africa. He came here looking for the right terroir. Bouchard Finlayson is such a special place and we thought we could make a difference – elevate it, make it better known, more accessible. So we invested. It's a work in progress all the time and I'm extremely proud and passionate about it and all that has been achieved over the last few years.'

Her sister, Toni, rushes into the stylish lounge of the new homestead that she built next to the cellar in 2007, furiously plumping cushions and rearranging Zulu baskets. An interior designer in Manhattan for 15 years, Toni now works in London. Why build a retro Cape Dutch farmhouse in the 21st century?

> 'We thought a homestead would be a good asset to promote our wines and wanted a venue that would be worthy of them. The homestead will be our showcase. We wanted it to be similar to the original Cape Dutch style homesteads, with walls of 600 mm thick. Wine tastes better in a beautiful environment and winemakers are poets. They need a sympathetic milieu to deliver their best. To decorate the house, I worked closely with Cape Town curator Michael Stevenson, and together we have assembled some great local art – both contemporary and older pieces from artists like Walter Oltmann and Hylton Nel.'

Is art important in Vicki's life? 'Art is a gift. It must be something I inherited. When my dad was 18 years old, he spent £5 buying two Irma Stern paintings.'

As Donald Hess has shown at Glen Carlou in Paarl, fine art and fine wine are a good match and a public art collection is yet another attraction for wine tourism, which is surely one of the most promising economic activities for the Western Cape. Through substantial investments upgrading the accommodation at Bushman's Kloof and ongoing developments at the Twelve Apostles Hotel and Spa, the Tollmans are obviously convinced by the Western Cape as a tourism destination. Vicki proudly adds:

> 'South Africa has such incredibly rich diversity. I want to impart some of this passion, to encourage tourism and change the perception of it being a third-world country, with no infrastructure or high level of service and standards.

On the drive from Cape Town, we stopped at a farm stall. Everything was so honest and authentic. Being involved in the hotel business I shouldn't really say this, but you don't need to stay in a five-star hotel to enjoy your stay. A good guesthouse or B&B can be a wonderful experience and sufficient. I'd rather have a smile than the silver service. We employ a lot of South Africans in our overseas hotels – their attitude is so refreshing. They're so hard-working, enthusiastic and are not jaded.'

Vicki's own inspiration comes from a close family: 'We try to make a difference to all our businesses, so they can be the best they can be. Our parents are our driving force, their dedication, passion and sincerity is what inspires us both.'

Having a father living in London is something Vicki shares with William Kentridge, the most successful South African-based artist to have emerged this generation. He kick-started a cellar by bartering art for wine with importer Michael Fridjhon, and recently added another 24 dozen bottles through another Fridjhon deal – offering six images from *Magic Flute* as wine labels. The deal went down at Ellerman House.

WILLIAM KENTRIDGE

William Kentridge has come a long way from those Paris goblets of box wine at exhibition openings at the Market Theatre. 'Johannesburg, Second-Greatest City after Paris', the title of his first animation work, was not a joke.

Reality imitated art at lunch in 2007 at Ellerman House in Bantry Bay. Hosting the meal of 'camembert, blueberry, asparagus and toasted pine nut salad with a blueberry dressing', to quote from the menu, followed by 'rare beef fillet with a Béarnaise sauce' and 'vanilla panna cotta with a hazelnut praline' was Paul Harris, who acquired control of Rand Merchant Bank in the mid-80s, along with G.T. Ferreira and Laurie Dippenaar.

RMB (motto: 'traditional values, innovative ideas') started making financial waves in Johannesburg around the time William Kentridge started drawing those apocalyptic images of his alter ego, Soho Eckstein – described by Susan Stewart in *The Open Studio: Essays on Art and Aesthetics* as a 'melancholy industrialist' – set in a blasted urban landscape that was to become the future of downtown Jo'burg.

So to have Paul and GT, plus Dave King, lunching in a Victorian mansion perched ballerina-like on Kloof Road above South Africa's own Côte d'Azur, not only located the centre of gravity of the *Sunday Times* rich list for a brief moment above Bantry Bay, but was also a piece of performance art: the heirs of Soho Eckstein dining with the artist.

By working with prints and films, Kentridge produces some of the most public art around. His latest project – bringing his production of Mozart's opera *The Magic Flute* to Johannesburg and Cape Town after a spring run in Brooklyn – is his most public one yet. The opera, which he designed and directed and for which he created projections and charcoal drawings, had its premiere in 2005 in Brussels at the Théatre de la Monnaie (Theatre at the Mint), a venue to warm the cockles of the heart of any Master of the Financial Universe.

To fund the *Flute*, Rand Merchant Bank has dug deep into its corporate pockets and played the role usually played by governments in Europe, which typically subsidise up to 75% of the cost of a ticket. As William noted, 'It will cost us a lot more than I expected – there were lots of complications and as a country, South Africa lacks the infrastructure to stage opera.' Producer Ross Douglas confirms the opera will cost R10 million to stage, with RMB sponsorship worth R2 million and Douglas hoping the state will come to the party.

To reach out to children, a condensed version of the production has been devised (slimmed down from three hours to one) that will be funded in large part by six wine producers who have each bought the rights to a charcoal for R50,000 (excluding VAT) for use as a wine label. A further two cases of wine from each producer will be signed by William and auctioned to raise additional cash. William and Ross get four dozen bottles from each producer for their time and effort, which will fit nicely into William's Houghton cellar and fuel his contention, 'I drink far better wine than I deserve.'

The project is the brainchild of Michael Fridjhon, one-time university debating partner of William and now visiting professor of wine marketing at UCT Business School and whose WineX shows (with performances twice a year in Cape Town and Johannesburg) have RMB as headline sponsor. Matching wine with the *Flute* makes total sense to William, who is interested in the whole winemaking process, 'which is one of transformation, changing grapes into wine'. Transformation is one of the themes of the *Flute*, which on one ridiculous level may be interpreted as the search by Papageno, a bird seller, for some decent wine.

This commodification of art into wine label is no new thing. America's arbiter of lifestyle issues, *Vanity Fair*, themed an entire edition to art, with Kentridge positioned close to the centre of the universe of fine art in a star chart of white dwarfs of drawing, planetoids of painting and comets of conceptual art.

Arty wine labels are nothing new – Château Mouton-Rothschild has famously commissioned a different artist to produce one for each vintage of its *grand vin* since 1945, and some of the gods of modern art, from Picasso to Bacon and Warhol and Ilya Kabakov, have been happy to accept the commission.

Of course, the *Vanity Fair* edition is not about art at all, but rather money, with the lead story, 'Money on the Wall', giving the game away. The title is a reference to Warhol's contention that rich folk should place montages of money on their walls as artworks so they can constantly see its value.

Something these lunch guests would never do, as cash is the ultimate bad investment: no dividend and easy to steal – far better off with art. As Dave King noted: 'Mark to market (with some issues about tradability), South African art was the best-performing investment in the world last year. I bought some (Gerard) Sekotos a few years ago and put them in my cellar, as I didn't really like them. Now that they've taken off, I've brought them up and show them with pride.'

An observation confirmed by João Ferreira of the eponymous Cape Town gallery, who confirms that 'prices have exploded, with artists like Maggie Laubser appreciating 1,000 per cent last year'. All good news for Dave, who set the local price record for Maggie a few years ago, with a purchase for R270,000.

In addition to Maggie and Gerard, Dave also collects Irma Stern and recounts how he was bidding for a work at Sotheby's in Rosebank, when someone at the back of the room started throwing pencils and paperclips at him. 'Your bidding technique consists of raising your arm and leaving it up,' interjects GT, 'so I had to get your attention somehow.' Well it worked, because consummate trader GT secured the work after the auction by offering Dave a 10 per cent premium on the hammer price.

Paul Harris has also been bitten by the art bug and is now driven by a desire to 'make something beautiful', hence his involvement in *The Magic Flute* sponsorship. His recent investment in the Everard Read Galleries confirms that having made his money in financial services, he intends to spend it elsewhere.

Opera also appeals to Dave, who used to be a patron of the State Opera in Pretoria – a venue that will not hear the *Flute*, as William admits: 'I prefer the Civic and we don't need two venues in Gauteng.' Dave's operatic highlight was to see Puccini's *Turandot* in the Forbidden City in Beijing a few years ago. After paying $500 for a ticket, he ended up seeing it twice after discovering that locals could buy tickets for $20 and were happy to sell them for $30 (adopting his on-selling Irma Stern approach).

Artists from Marc Chagall to David Hockney have been inspired by the *Flute*. William chose it 'because it's so open-ended in terms of visual language. It raises questions of colonialism and issues around people believing in the certainty of possessing a monopoly on truth.'

The Manichaean German intellectual framework is also a comfortable fit for this great-grandson of Jewish immigrants from Lithuania, 'who changed their name from Kantorovitch to Kentridge in an attempt to fit in'. As is his famously monochrome palette, which will be somewhat relieved and coloured through lighting effects designed by Jennifer Tipton.

While William can feel 'the weight of European tradition and thoughts pressing down on us here at the southern tip', that certainly does not mean that eighteenth-century Austrians have a monopoly on his inspiration. 'More operas than ever are being written today,' he reflects, 'and more old operas are being performed. I'd love to direct one by Tom Waits or Laurie Anderson.'

The six wineries participating in the *Magic Flute* project represent the *tête du cuvée* of South African wine. Rustenberg in Stellenbosch has been dubbed 'the quintessential South African wine estate' by Anthony Hamilton Russell, whose own specialty is making Burgundian-inspired reds and elegant whites at Walker Bay. Rustenberg's then winemaker, Adi Badenhorst, had recently been invited to join the Cape Winemakers' Guild, so owner Simon Barlow thought his charcoal rhinoceros would suit a CWG wine.

Images were assigned to wines by picking names out of William's trademark panama hat. A possibility of exchange saw 'Hammo' swapping his for a landscape to fit in with the classical nature of his wines and his own love of that genre. Thereby confirming that cartoonist Bill Watterson was not entirely joking when he had Calvin and Hobbes comment in mind: 'Art has no purpose. All that's left is commodity marketing. Consequently, I'm signing this landscape and you can own it for a million dollars.'

Fate dealt eighth-generation Meerlust owner Hannes Myburgh a pyramid with a Masonic eye on top, a bit like an armed response sign. Or a lighthouse (which is quite appropriate, as Meerlust is close to False Bay). Hannes thinks he'll use it for his 2004 Meerlust Cabernet Sauvignon.

Marc Kent from Boekenhoutskloof is a master of Syrah and has started collecting art by contemporary artists like Joachim Schönfeldt. He was thrilled with his bird image. Ditto for Dave and his Quoin Rock wines, while GT decided to go with the image Rand Merchant Bank has adopted as logo for the opera, for his Tokara wines.

GT says he enjoys 'the tactile aspect of winemaking', after a career juggling numbers. He relates how he was once asked what he did. 'Retired banker turned wine farmer,' was his reply.

'Show me your hands. There are no calluses, so you're clearly not much of a farmer,' was the verdict.

'But I do have a callus on my finger from writing all the cheques,' shot back GT. With his new Tokara label, he can now add 'patron of the opera' to his CV.

Someone with real calluses on her hands is Marlene Dumas, who grew up on Jacobsdal wine farm in Stellenbosch. When her brother, Cornelis, went to Amsterdam on a Cape Legends roadshow to promote his wine, I decided to tag along.

PROTECTING PURITY: MARLENE DUMAS

Cornelis Dumas makes a deeply traditional Pinotage in cement vats on the edge of the Cape Flats. His sister is one of the superstars of modern art.

'Words and images drink the
same wine.
There is no purity to protect.'

(MARLENE DUMAS, *Sweet Nothings*)

Fine art and fine wine are in the news a lot, mostly for all the wrong reasons. A recent run of comet vintages in Bordeaux has seen wines offered *en primeur* (ie while still in the barrel) at stellar prices to the global network of merchants and traders who lubricate the supply pipeline from cellars to restaurants, retailers and consumers.

Prices have flown off the scale. A case of Bordeaux's finest, Château Latour, is likely to set you back £4,000 by the time it's finally released. It's the same story with art, with a portrait of Adele Bloch-Bauer by Gustav Klimt sold to a cosmetics mogul for $135 million. Which comes as no surprise, as it's often the same individuals who are buying the wine and the art.

What is remarkable is how the nouveau riche billionaires of Russia and Asia have swallowed the marketing spiel of European consumerism and now aspire to Western icons, whether it be Picasso or Pétrus, Kirwan or Klimt. A point well made by South African-born artist Marlene Dumas, who now lives and works in Amsterdam.

In the catalogue to the exhibition 'MD' she notes: 'But you tell me – why on earth should I instinctively prefer the Greeks to the Colombians? Why should I prefer the Great American Nude to the early Taoist love manuals and why am I supposed to feel closer to Leda and the Swan than Japanese shunga?'

It's the same story with wine, when the Chinese give free farms to the Bordelais in exchange for know-how and cuttings from their vines, rather than developing their own indigenous varieties, like Baiyu ('white feather') and Longyan ('dragon's eye'). At the southernmost tip, that barber-surgeon Jan van Riebeeck ordered out for European vines to be planted. Just as well, some would say – Louis Leipoldt described the indigenous Gros Colman grape as 'sour as vinegar and possessed of a pip that burns your tongue like a chilli!'.

But there is a uniquely South African grape of great potential, albeit a crossing of two Old World cultivars – Pinotage. Marlene's brother, Cornelis, makes wines from it of great character, brimming with a sense of place, on the family farm Jacobsdal. When you drink them in Europe, your palate tells you they're 'not from here', which was the title of Marlene's first exhibition in the USA.

Marlene has also been in the news quite a bit: for the record price achieved by a living female artist and for making it into *Art-Review* magazine's power 100 list of movers and shakers in the art world. I'm tempted to add that the first must irritate her intensely – being reported purely for the price her work achieves. Remember the essay of her friend, the South African novelist Marlene van Niekerk, printed in the catalogue of Dumas's 2005 show at the Zwirner & Wirth Gallery in New York: 'I write about my own work because I want to speak for myself. I might not be the only authority, or the best authority, but I want to participate in the writing of my own history . . . I don't like being paternalised and colonised by every Tom, Dick and Harry that comes along (male or female).'

What follows is a conversation between Marlene, Cornelis and me that took place at Studio Dumas in Amsterdam in 2007. An edited version appeared in the *Sunday Times Lifestyle*.

The sign for Studio Dumas is small, discreet (like the sign for Jacobsdal, 10,000 km to the south, on the shore of the Cape Flats). It's a five-letter plaque, like a box of expensive cigarettes viewed side-on. Blink and you'd miss them both. 'But I do wish you'd been late,' were Marlene's first words as she flung open the front door, curly red hair like an explosion in an autumn mattress factory. 'I have to write fifty words on Marlene van Niekerk and it has to be done today.'

Inside, the spacious studio with four large rooms doesn't seem at all Dutch. Outside, a garden with a wooden fence that separates this former photographer's studio from an art facility next door for people with mental handicaps. There's a grapevine in the corner. 'Looks like Cabernet,' comments Cornelis.

'This is my third trip overseas,' he laughs. 'The first was a two-week honeymoon in Rio. We got so suntanned that when we left, the Brazilian immigration officials moved us to the queue for Brazilians to board the plane. 1999 was the first time I came to Amsterdam and Marlene was living on two houseboats on a canal. She still has them.'

'Something to drink? I went to the supermarket to buy some South African wine', she says, pointing to the bottle of 1652 Sauvignon Blanc on the counter – one of those cheap and cheerful South African no-name wines so popular in fiscally prudent Holland – and historically impossible, as Jan van Riebeeck didn't start importing vines until 1655. 'That was all I could find. Is it any good, Boeta?'

We settle for a bottle of Chardonnay from the Languedoc in the fridge, which ends up in the sink when Marlene produces a Laurent Perrier champagne with a flourish. 'I got this from my Belgian gallerist, so it should be OK. I don't work with "dealers" – they only sell and buy. Gallerists work with you through periods of thick and thin. It's a very different relationship. Gallerists hate dealers and Belgians always feel they have better taste in wine and food than the Dutch.'

The first room is full of metal racks stuffed with books. 'For me, making an exhibition is like writing a book – I've always wanted to write a book – and it's an important point of difference with some other painters. Everyone can paint a painting, but do you have a philosophy? All better painters have a philosophy – they don't paint pictures, they try to express a moral and aesthetic point of view.'

A point made in a non-verbal fashion by Cornelis, who is one of the most revolutionary winemakers in the Cape. Like a rock in False Bay, the waves of wine fashion break over this farmer, who has been making 'the same wine for thirty years'.

'Like I've been painting the same themes for thirty years,' adds Marlene. 'Art is a visual process, but without the actual work seen, you end up talking about reproduction, which takes away texture, scale and context. With wine, you drink the thing and there's more to go round! A wine critic will (hopefully) never write about a wine he has never drunk, while with visual art people write about works they've never seen. With wine, there are many bottles of the same wine. Not so with paintings.'

With great faith in the uniquely South African grape Pinotage – the butt of many jokes in snooty wine-writing circles – Cornelis is deeply traditional, making it in concrete *kuipe* (vats). 'A well-known winemaker used to visit and kept telling me to pump my juice over. My workers used to call him *Mr Oorpomp* [a bit of a rude joke as the man in question fancies himself as something of a lothario]. I just leave the wine. I don't even add yeast. I let it do its own thing.

'When I was in Sweden, they asked me: "Isn't it very boring to make the same wine year in, year out?" But it's never the same thing. Each year is different.'

'Cornelis works with nature and I too work with chance. I want to make the erotic painting. I want to make the painting about death. But I also want to be surprised. It's a question of concentration and being aware.'

'I pick the grapes earlier or later, depending on the weather, then I blend . . . '

'It's not a glamorous process, you know, this making art. In fact it's extremely unglamorous. I paint on the floor and have to go down on my knees to make a painting, literally and figuratively.'

'It's just like I make wine,' laughs Cornelis. 'It's a struggle.'

Conversation with the Dumas duo is a hectic affair: they both speak at the same time, volumes rising as they get fired up.

'The whole family is like this. It's always been hectic. My dad died when I was 21 – I was still at varsity and Marlene was 12. I was the oldest, so I became the farmer. My middle brother, Pieter, was no good with his hands. He became a *dominee*. Marlene was Dad's favourite. She was always an artist. When we went to the Kruger Park, my dad said it was a waste of time taking Marlene, as she would sit in the back, drawing on the back of a cigarette box. She didn't look out the window once.

'If my wine is not ready, I hold it back. You can't sell someone a bottle of wine and expect them to keep it for five years before they can drink it.'

'Sometimes my paintings aren't ready for me. Sometimes I'm not ready for a painting. I keep it and in five years, maybe it falls into place. It's a non-linear world view, a much more holistic view of looking at things.'

'I've always wanted the best for my wine, that's why I went with Distell [the largest liquor corporate in South Africa] to bottle, market and distribute my wines.'

'I don't make art so that I can be remembered when I'm dead.

Some works are of shorter duration than others. But it's hard to judge. Figurative art is difficult if the subject is sensational.' (Portraits of Osama Bin Laden, Timothy McVeigh and Mohammed Bouyeri, who stabbed film-maker Theo van Gogh (grand-grand-nephew of Vincent) to death on an Amsterdam street in 2002, glower darkly in the studio.) 'Looking back, you can see differences. You need the distance that time gives.'

'It's the same with wine. I am always surprised at how long some wines last, like my '86. My grandfather started the farm and my son, Hannes, will take it over.'

'Our dad never entered wine competitions,' interjects Marlene.

'I don't make wine for publicity either, but I am always glad when we get it. I must say, I did like winning a gold medal at Vinexpo [the huge biennial wine show held in Bordeaux] – although the wine which won wasn't my best wine and it didn't last as long as expected.'

'Creativity keeps you humble. Critics are important. Even the negative ones, but then they must explain their comments. I'm against gratuitous negative bashing. What can you do when someone says, "she would be nothing if she wasn't a woman . . . " There's not much I can do about that.' Fine art and fine wine may both be controlled by a powerful circle of critics. 'But the wheel turns. Look at Clement Greenberg. Later on, he was so crushed . . . '

'[A well-known South African wine writer] liked teasing me. He kept repeating that I was making what I called "the national red drinking wine, Pinotage" since 1966. What I meant was that Pinotage had the potential to make a great South African wine. I don't care who makes it.'

'You just need to live long enough to see the world change,' adds Marlene. Isn't fine art, like fine wine, becoming too expensive, too decadent, the plaything of rich people? 'But I don't want to own my own paintings. I like museums, I'm a big fan. People can see art in museums. Private ownership is not essential, although a true lover is wonderful to find.'

'I've paid my dues,' continues Marlene. 'While some of my friends married swimming pools, I lived with my clothes in boxes. To make a show I work for a year and produce a series of works, which, all together, suggest a story. A commentary on how one looks at things. Not that you're making a decoration – that's not my aim – but that said, I'm not against craft – we are folkloristic. I don't exclude a non-expert audience. I don't do it for the people and I don't do it against the people. If at all, I do it from the people and after the people. Since becoming a professional artist, I've never entered competitions myself, although I have accepted prizes given to me.'

'It's the same for me,' agrees Cornelis. 'You need your own values. I don't make show wines for so-called experts.'

'I came to Holland when I was 23.'

'And I started making wine when I was 21.'

'I was at art school in Cape Town in the 70s. I didn't go away to go away . . . '

'I can't get away from my wine. I'd much rather be back on my farm, making wine, than travelling in Europe.'

'And I can't get away from art . . . we're caught in a trap; we can't look back . . . ' Marlene starts singing Elvis. 'Before I left South Africa, an American photographer told me, "You'll get lost in a supermarket." And here I sit, *kan nie fiets nie, kan nie swem nie, kan nie kar ry ni*e [can't ride a bike, can't swim, can't drive a car]. I've become like my dad, short and round. My mom was the elegant one. It was all a surprise to me. I still can't speak proper Dutch and I've been here for 30 years. Dutch feels pompous to me because my mother tongue is Afrikaans. I like the beat of Afrikaans more than Dutch. It's like slang, it moves faster. I travel a lot by taxi and because most taxi drivers are also not originally from here, we talk and laugh about language and its differences.'

'When my dad died so young, I had to become a farmer. It was terribly difficult. It was the time of sanctions. Red wine was not in great demand locally. Jacobsdal is situated on the extreme southwesterly edge of the Stellenbosch wine region. There's no water. It's the wine farm that shouldn't exist. But it's still mine. Today, I'm both farmer and winemaker.'

'I never called myself an artist for a long time. I never thought I was good enough,' confesses Marlene.

'But we're very determined people,' responds Cornelis.

And has she now arrived? 'No, never,' she howls. 'Time feels so short.'

'We're still doing what we like. I survived, but I'm still not open to the public and only give tastings by prior arrangement in the homestead.'

'It's true, you can't make art and entertain people at the same time,' his sister agrees. 'It's a new tourism – intellectual tourism. Collectors want to spend time with you. The artist Louise Bourgeoise got so agitated, she broke a sculpture during a TV interview. The whole thing is so scrambled. Do you want a facelift or do you want to colour your hair?'

'I had to turn away a whole busload of Germans who arrived to visit the farm after I had said I was busy. I was in my shorts, covered in grape skins. I was making wine and didn't have the time. But everyone wants to meet the owner, to talk to the winemaker.'

'Often I'm like a stand-up comedian when I give lectures. The Americans wanted to see me in person. I had an exhibition in Chicago on death, after Bush had invaded Iraq. I didn't want to go, so I made a video. "Oh no, you must come!" they said. "We don't like Bush either." So I went and commented on myself as my works appeared on the video. When it finished, I asked if they wanted to see my slides about my sex-related works. They were relieved.'

Marketing mojo

Selling the stuff is the crucial last link in the chain between vineyard and consumer. Stuff it up, and the result, as Mr Micawber said, is misery. With many thousands of local and international wines available to oenophiles, marketing has never been as important.

If people look increasingly like their pets with age, that winemakers should look like their wines should come as no surprise. Along with blockbuster drops with huge alcohols, South Africa also produces some of the biggest winemakers in the world. Karl Lambour now makes an elegantly green Sauvignon Blanc at Constantia Glen, but back in his days when he was setting Fleur du Cap on the glittering path to vinous stardom, he was described by this rookie wine writer as: 'More than two metres tall and built like a brick public convenience, Lambour would win a double gold medal for size in any anthropometric competition.' Fortunately, this was one gentle giant who didn't take offence.

Over in Franschhoek the even more massive Niël Groenewald makes Bellingham's exotic Fair Maiden, a Rhônish blend of Chenin Blanc, Chardonnay, Verdelho, Rousanne, Viognier and Grenache Blanc. But his real forte is as a carnivore: at the London Wine Trade Fair he is the undisputed steak-eating champion, calling for thirds while little Aussie battlers struggle through their firsts.

Donovan Rall comes from the same Brobdingnagian stock. Deputy manager at the Bottelary Hills Wine Centre in Stellenbosch, he qualified as a winemaker at the University of Stellenbosch and yet here he is, selling wine. His reason is compelling:

> 'South Africa produces over one hundred winemakers a year and there aren't jobs for them all, so after graduating, I went overseas. I started out at Harrods in London and ended up at Harvey Nichols, a department store in Knightsbridge.

While I was studying I worked at South African wineries like Tokara and also Cloudy Bay in New Zealand, but I thought I'd rather make a career in marketing and retail. After all, if you make the best wine in the world and can't sell it, what's the point?'

As Frank Sinatra sang of New York, 'if you can make it there, you'll make it anywhere', a sentiment taken to heart by Mark Solms.

FIRST WE TAKE MANHATTAN

The centre of the financial universe is as good a place as any to start.

'They sentenced me to twenty years of boredom
For trying to change the system from within
I'm coming now, I'm coming to reward them
First we take Manhattan, then we take Berlin.'

(LEONARD COHEN, *First We Take Manhattan*)

Leonard Cohen could have had Mark Solms in mind when he penned the lyrics of the opening song to his 1988 album, *I'm Your Man*. At the risk of over-egging the barrel, South African wine was a seriously boring story before Mark Solms arrived with his desiccated grapes and Museum van de Caab, which connected South African wine to its cultural history for the first time. Sure, Groot Constantia, Nederburg and Meerlust had told the white side of the story for decades, but Solms was the first to present the whole picture.

Professor Solms now looks to be rewriting the wine marketing book as well, acquiring shelf space in some of Manhattan's most prestigious retail outlets for his brand. Sherry-Lehmann Wine & Spirits on the Upper East Side is the refuelling outlet for the dowagers and billionaires with apartments overlooking Central Park

– the owners of those poodles you see taking their chauffeurs for a walk. It is located on Park Avenue, and you need to take care when browsing in Sherry that your 'famous blue raincoat' does not bum-brush a stand of Pétrus.

The Sherry selection of South African wine is idiosyncratic, to say the least. The last time I was there was to load up on Excelsior Cabernet Sauvignon at $9.99 a bottle for casual quaffing. This was the previous vintage of the 'always reliable' wine, demoted from three to one-and-a-half stars in the 2008 edition of Platter's (an assessment, I hear, that was embarrassingly reversed when publisher, editor and a couple of assorted Platter's palates tasted the wine again recently). This time, the assessment was done blind and the Excelsior was judged three stars, unlike a couple of other Cabernets that had been rated sighted at three but collapsed to two when done blind. Now we know why the guide has a red cover for 2008!

Joining the Excelsior on the Sherry shelf will be Solms's Koloni and Africana, both wines under the Solms-Hegewisch brand, a desiccated white and red respectively, made by Hilko Hegewisch. Over at Rockefeller Plaza, Wall Street Masters of the Universe will be able to order Solms-Delta wines with their pastrami on rye at the Morrel & Co. wine bar, while the marvellously named Frankly Wines on Broadway and Gnarly Vines in Brooklyn will offer Hier-vandaan and Lekkerwijn, both guaranteed tongue-twisters for noo-yawk tawkers.

Less of a surprise is the listing at Astor Wine & Spirits on Lafay-ette Street. After all, Richard Astor is a partner and his ancestor, John Jacob Astor, just about owned Manhattan in the late eigh-teenth century, lending his name to the famous Waldorf-Astoria hotel. Stand by for a Solms-Astor listing there too. Vastrap would be most appropriate, even if it's been a long time since a mud and manure floor had to be danced flat in Manhattan.

Cohen's advice to start with Manhattan before tackling Ber-lin is not universally accepted. A letter to the editor of *WineLand* magazine by WOSA's Dalene Steyn is something of a report back

on the recent VinPro Information Day held at Goudini Spa. Ms
Steyn reports:

> 'While Johan Bruwer's point that there is still a lot of scope
> for South Africa in the United States is well made, his com-
> ments were very valid, but I believe we need to be cautious.

> 'While exploring the American market and tapping into its
> potential is a positive step for those producers who can afford
> to sustain a long-term marketing campaign and make inroads
> into this highly competitive market, the majority of South
> African producers would be better serviced by continuing to
> build and maintain their marketing bases in Europe.

> 'This is especially pertinent in view of the fact that California
> is increasing its efforts and budget to grow market share in
> Europe. Not being able to predict if a recession will actually
> happen in the States, it may well be cheaper to defend mar-
> ket share in Europe than open the US market.'

Su Birch, CEO of WOSA, agrees with Steyn:

> 'There has been a huge consolidation of distributors in the
> United States and the road is littered with very expensive
> failures. Most South African producers underestimate the
> resources required. There is not even a South African cat-
> egory in the United States and we need a generic marketing
> campaign to generate awareness. The United States is the
> fastest-growing market and is clearly the place to be, but
> WOSA does not have the resources required. It is a lot easier
> to sell wine in other parts of the world.'

Reacting to Steyn's letter and a January report in *Decanter* that
America will soon become the largest wine consumer in the world,

Andre Shearer, CEO of Cape Classics, the largest, oldest and arguably most successful South African wine merchant in the United
States, begged to differ:

> 'Who on earth would not want to be part of that? Now, if South
> African producers are being advised by a formal wine industry
> body to avoid the United States, they'd be plain stupid. If they
> are suggesting that you'd better have your best juice, best funds,
> best marketing hat and masses of long-term energy – they'd be
> right. The United States has higher standards than our other
> export markets and, therefore, only the best survive. We should
> be raising our standards vigorously instead of running to the
> less difficult, but lower barrier to entry markets. That being
> said, in a free market, go where you go and do what you do.

> 'I would urge South African producers to continue to refine
> their viticultural skills, make ripe wines with finesse, and get
> serious about collaboration so that we can jointly raise our
> overall standards and not settle for grand mediocrity, which
> I still believe is very prevalent. We are just very, very lucky
> that our region produces nice wines with some effort. I do
> not mean that people don't work hard, but I do think we
> need to work a lot smarter, to coin an American phrase. I
> still believe totally that the United States will still ultimately
> define what great South African wine is.'

With WOSA and Shearer offering diverging opinions, the conflict-
ing signals sent to producers are confusing, to say the least. Perhaps
Solms has a solution – do it yourself. As Cohen summed it up:

> 'I'm guided by a signal in the heavens
> I'm guided by this birthmark on my skin
> I'm guided by the beauty of our weapons
> First we take Manhattan, then we take Berlin.'

SENSORY MARKETING

Wine is food. Wine is a drug. Wine is sophisticated, fashionable, complex. A worthy subject for the most audacious, big and hairy marketing strategies.

Telesales calls when you're in the shower and coat hanger vendors at the traffic intersection are just two of the 5,000-odd commercial messages we are exposed to every day. TV, radio, billboards, computer screen pop-ups, junk email and cell phone spam text messages, slogans on windcheaters, shoes and shopping bags are all part of the $244 billion advertising industry (2003 figures) beavering away to sell you something you don't need.

On the face of it a thriving industry, but scratch a little deeper and it's crisis time for creative directors. Around 20 per cent of US households now have access to technology to edit out TV ads. More than two-thirds of American magazines have to live with falling circulation figures. Newspaper sales in the UK are on an inexorable slide. The fast-forward button on the DVD player now skips over the traditional 30 minutes of cinema advertisements and future attractions in a flash.

Anti-spam software and consumer legislation designed to limit junk post and the promotion of tobacco and alcohol are popular initiatives, which together conspire to make the job of the twenty-first century ad-exec that little bit more challenging. So a call goes out for a latter-day superhero – the international marketing consultant. Like Martin Lindstrom, a 'brand futurist' with a CV that comes in five different sizes, ranging from ultrashort (listed as 24 words, although actually 43 words long), short, medium and extensive, all the way through to 'comprehensive' at 458 words (which could be whittled down to 457 if Pepsi were not listed twice on the 'blue-chip client list'). Or could this be a postmodern marketing ploy, like misspelling your brand name to stop speed readers in their tracks?

From the XXL CV, we learn that Lindstrom got into marketing at an early age after being declared the best Lego builder in Denmark, Lego being the greatest Danish contribution to the jollity of nations since the Vikings and Hans Christian Andersen, whose bicentenary the Danes celebrated with firework parties and the inauguration of a walk around Copenhagen allowing tourists to retrace the footsteps of the great man by following size 14 footprints painted onto city pavements. (Although the walking trail was somewhat compromised by pranksters with their own footprint stencil leading tourists on unexpected detours to the Museum of Erotica and diverse unsavoury cellar bars.)

As national Lego champion, Lindstrom developed a Legoland in the back garden of his home on the island of Jutland, which in the first year of opening had over 1,000 paying visitors (admission R25) or nearly 3 people a day. Lindstrom Legoland added another attraction to Jutland, site of the great World War I naval battle.

European child labour laws notwithstanding, Lindstrom was hired by Lego as a designer at the tender age of 12 and concurrently established a marketing company to promote his mother's beauty products. The products must have been amazing, as his client list soon included Disney, McDonald's, Pepsi, Mars Bars and M&Ms – dream clients for a preteen, or 'tweenager' as he prefers to call the 8–14 year-old age cohort.

Lindstrom soon attracted the attention of mainstream Danish advertising executives and was offered a job by no fewer than seven different agencies – so he used astrology to choose BBDO, using the natal charts of the seven companies, a suitably more exotic criterion than enquiring who offered the best salary and conditions.

By the age of 30, this super-Scandinavian was COO of British Telecom/LookSmart, and he now travels the world on a perpetual pilgrimage of marketing: 49 cities in 29 countries, so no surprises when the Lindstrom roadshow hit Johannesburg and Cape Town with its message of sensory marketing. The *Financial Times* described Lindstrom as 'a skinny, blond smudge in black shirt, black trousers and black shoes'; his own website claims that as a speaker, he is 'guaranteed a standing ovation', with lack of self-confidence and false modesty clearly not an issue.

The Lindstrom marketing mantra is a simple one which came to him literally by accident in Tokyo, when he bumped into a mama-san. Her perfume was so distinctive, he immediately went and bought a bottle. An accident which marked the birth of sensory marketing – the idea that advertisements should address all five senses, rather than the conventional two-dimensional approach targeted at sight and sound. His latest book, *Brand Sense* (Free Press, 2005), is full of examples and well worth the price. A free chapter is downloadable from his website (www.martinlindstrom.com).

If you accept Lindstrom's proposition that 'almost our entire understanding of the world is experienced through our senses' – perhaps delete the 'almost', as the case for extrasensory perception has not yet been made – then the senses are the channels a marketer must target, in fact they are the only ones available. And some brands do it better than others.

Take sound, for example. Cereal colossus Kellogg engaged a Danish commercial music laboratory to design the optimal crunch for cornflakes – a crunch the company is keen on patenting. Or Daimler Chrysler, makers of Mercedes Benz, who employed a team of engineers to analyse and create the perfect sound of a car door opening and closing. (Which speaks volumes about the current problems of the automobile industry and the outrageous cost of cars.)

Smell is another fruitful field of market research for car manufacturers, following a study that it is a new car smell rather than mileage or performance that defines a new car for potential purchasers. Another branch of the travel industry, Singapore Airlines, even patented the smell of their airline cabins, which are doused with a fragrance, which has the very un-Asian name of Stefan Floridian Waters. From freshen-up towels to air hostess perfume, SFW is an integral part of the airline's brand. Although becoming a Singapore Girl is harder to do than booking a Voyager ticket in December – the uniform comes in just one size and retirement arrives early at the tender age of 26.

Of all consumer commodities wine is the best fit for Lindstrom's sensory marketing and faced with a glut of 27 million litres of unsold red, Cape winemakers should make attentive students.

Starting with sight, packaging is clearly a predominantly visual application: the bottle shape is part of the Grünberger Stein brand, as Checkers found out when the retailer appropriated the *bocksbeutel* (German for goat's scrotum) for their Muchas Gracias brand, starting up a dispute that went all the way to the Supreme Court and ended with a judgment that is perpetually on appeal. Other famous bottle shapes include DGB's Bellingham Johannisberger, based on a mountain in Franschhoek behind the Bellingham farm where Niël Groenewald does his magic. Similarly, Pongraçz comes in a bottle by no coincidence the same shape as the one used by Krug, an iconic French fizz with a German name (as they usually are, not so, Mr Heidsieck?).

Colour can also be an important brand cue, as the precise shade of ochre patented by Veuve Clicquot for their misnamed Yellow Label brand of bubbly confirms. On the local scene, Giorgio Dalla Cia's Bordeaux blend called Giorgio comes in a most fetching shade of papal purple. Clearly someone took Gogol Bordello's injuncture to "wear purple" seriously. Distell's latest range of concept wines, called Flat Roof Manor, are colour coded with a northern Californian palette of taupe, beige, burnt umber and sienna, while Platter's pundit Irina von Holdt's blue bottles of Blue White Chenin Blanc are unmistakable cultural artefacts from the 90s.

Visual cues are an oft underrated part of wine appreciation. If Austrian glassmaker Georg Riedel had his way, they'd remain so, with his selection of black glasses – ranging in price from $20 for a black, stemless Chardonnay tumbler to $30 for a Cabernet glass – doing a brisk trade on Amazon.com. Although quite why you'd want to drink Montrachet from a black tumbler is a moot point.

Aroma (bouquet), taste and touch (mouth feel) are the obvious trio of organoleptic options addressed at wine shows and in-store tastings, although being 10,000 times more sensitive than taste, smell is seriously underutilised. If supermarkets can duct and channel the smell of baking bread throughout a store to increase sales, wineries should make use of that romantic aroma of wooden barrels, spilt wine, mould and damp that makes a visit to a cellar in Burgundy so atmospheric.

Hearing is a less obvious marketing option: the sound of wine being poured is fairly generic, while the sub-Vivaldi theme tune of South Africa's largest wine brand, Nederburg, no longer fits its more youthful image. Perhaps the most exciting auditory application is the talking wine label. Commercial messages that emanate from store-front panes when a consumer is within listening distance – whispering windows – are a reality. Now, Italian label manufacturer Modulgraf has proposed a plastic label that can be read like a CD. Customers armed with label readers will be able to scan the serried bottles and hear assorted winemakers whisper sweet nothings, which should make some cuvées, like a Pinot Noir from Anthony Hamilton Russell, even more irresistible.

Marketing is essentially the manipulation of the masses, and a staff writer on *The New Yorker*, James Surowiecki, offers a lot for wine marketers to think about.

THE WISDOM OF CROWDS

Everyone's opinion can contribute to choosing wine. It's a party and everyone's invited.

Googlefight is the techie alternative to Veritas, the national wine show. Input two contenders into an idiot-proof GUI, hit the 'make a fight' button and the collective wisdom of the worldwide web will deliver its verdict in a nanosecond or two using the Google Internet search engine to tally the number of hits for each candidate. Broadband rapid response is a pity, as while the search engine interrogates the net, Keith Haring-style cartoon characters act out a boxing match with lots of biffs, thumps and vibrating parentheses.

Looking for the Cape's first icon wine? Propose 'Meerlust Rubicon' and 'Vergelegen V' and Googlefight hands the laurels to the latter by 13,300 hits to 9,620. Cabernet Sauvignon v. Pinot Noir? It's Bordeaux over Burgundy by 1,070,000 to 925,000. How does local hero Pinotage rate against Uruguayan heart-throb Tannat? It's the Springboks versus the Pumas again, with South Africa victorious by 183,000 to 61,300 (although the Argentinians would do somewhat better if they fielded Malbec, with 435,000 hits).

Googlefight is an entertaining example of harnessing the wisdom of crowds, which, according to Surowiecki, author of the book by the same name (Abacus, 2005), is a smart (and free) way to solve a problem. This deceptively simple idea, that large groups of people are smarter than an elite few – no matter how gifted – has profound implications for wine competitions and restaurant and wine guides. Of course, as with most good ideas, this one would not have surprised Plato or Socrates, since participatory democracy in ancient Greece was extended to all civic decisions (slaves and women excepted).

The vinous analogy is that public opinion at wine shows, like those of Juliet Cullinan or Michael Fridjhon's WineX, produces a result far more reliable than the 15 tasters for the annual Platter's wine guide, judging panels of wine competitions or a Cape Wine Master AGM. Furthermore, this way the dreaded conflict of interest conundrum, which tarnishes so much informed opinion in the gustatory arts, is neatly avoided.

As noted in its introduction, the website www.winedemocracy.com proclaims that 'the most effective way to restrict democracy is to transfer decision making from the public arena to unaccountable institutions: kings and princes, party dictatorships, or professional wine critics'.

When the curtain descends on the annual Platter tasting

marathon and the spittoons are emptied and around 5,000 empty
bottles are carted off for recycling, then arguments about the pros
and cons of blind tasting come to the fore (Googlefight prefers
blind to sighted tasting by a margin of better than 10:1). Each camp
has a string of arguments nearly as numerous as the styles of Riedel
glasses, but perhaps the worst feature of sighted tastings is that producers are asked to supply a list of awards already achieved by the
wine – leading to a second-order effect that a wine becomes famous
for being famous. Which signposts the slippery slope to celebrity
cuvées like those of Mexican guitar god Carlos Santana, perpetual
bachelor boy Cliff Richard and the 'big easy', Ernie Els.

While vertiginous vineyards can make great wine, when it comes
to ranking them, the playing fields need to be level. But with many
producers such as Springfield and Thelema still resisting the siren
calls of pricey wine shows (Meerlust eventually caved in after much
soul-searching by Hannes Myburgh), track records are necessarily
biased to favour those with deep marketing pockets, long arms and
faith in the show system. Far better for tasters to make up their own
minds and risk being ridiculed for rubbishing a Toasty winner or
boosting a Veritas non-medalist (a *rara avis* indeed) to the rafters.
In effect, leaving it to the wisdom of crowds.

Deep down, everybody resents an expert, especially a wine pundit. As we've already noted, the *London Review of Books* commented: 'Common sense has always suspected that connoisseurship was
just snobbery tricked out as expertise, and that wine connoisseurship was one of the purest forms of pretence.' Surowiecki supplies
an alternative with a seductive pseudoscientific explanation of why
you're better off asking a bunch of people how many jellybeans are
in a jar and then averaging the answers, rather than phoning the
friendly MD of Beacon Sweets for his opinion.

Points are made and proved by anecdotes – locating a sunken US
navy submarine; the behaviour of the stock prices of the companies
that built the space shuttle after the Challenger exploded; why an
Internet search engine called Google is worth more than the GDPs

of some medium-size countries – and a deeper truth is teased out from these disparate incidents. Expert opinion is often unreliable and you're usually better off asking the opinion of a crowd. 'If you want to make a correct decision or solve a problem, large groups of people are smarter than a few experts,' says Surowiecki (although this algorithm clearly failed on the question of whether the earth was flat in pre-Renaissance times. A point renegade theologian Hans Küng uses to challenge the doctrine of papal infallibility – the Pope got it wrong with Galileo).

But it certainly works for Google, which reckons the more people that visit an Internet page, the more authoritative it is – a business model that made the company worth more than Time Warner. The wisdom of crowds is also used by epicurious.com ('the world's greatest recipe collection'), which awards recipes a number of forks according to their popularity. The star ratings of titles on Amazon. com are also a crowd response, even if many of the rave reviews are contributed by the very authors of the books themselves, under assumed personae.

Another drawback to picking by poll is the self-perpetuating nature of choosing something because other people buy it, the success of the Harry Potter novels and Dan Brown's *The Da Vinci Code* being salutary cases in point. But like it or not, more and more choices are being made on the basis of rankings.

Surowiecki's requirements for a smart crowd are simple:

1. The crowd should be diverse.
2. The crowd should be decentralised so no individual can coordinate responses.
3. Opinions must be summarised into a collective verdict.
4. Members of the crowd should be independent.

Which is a given at most wine festivals. Surowiecki himself is no ivory tower expert with extravagant forests of ear hair and a garish bow tie, but rather a staff writer at *The New Yorker* where he handles the business column. *The New Yorker* is a fertile growth medium for popular psychology. Another staff member, Malcolm Gladwell, supplies further insight into how best to choose your hedonistic poison in his latest opus, *Blink: the Power of Thinking Without Thinking* (Little, Brown & Co., 2005), a book that explains why your first impressions are often your best impressions.

How many times have you pondered a glass of wine, thought, 'Ha! Cheap Hanepoot' and then proceeded to convince yourself it was Château Climens (or, embarrassingly, vice versa). Corporate America has given Gladwell the blink of approval and companies like HP queue to pay him $45,000 a lecture to avoid reading the book (in itself, a good example of the blink phenomenon).

Gladwell is no newcomer to the self-help shelves. With a retro afro and a website (www.Gladwell.com), he started off with scoops in *The New Yorker*, such as 'True Colors: Hair Dye and the Hidden History of Post-war America' and 'The Ketchup Conundrum – If Mustard Comes in Dozens of Varieties, Why has Ketchup Stayed the Same?'. His first serious wave was caused by his book *The Tipping Point* (Back Bay, 2002), a sort of dumbed-down cultural catastrophe theory dealing with how situations (epidemics, stock prices, wars and fads) reach a tipping point before spiralling out of control. A prolific contributor to the corporate lexicon ('core competencies' and 'going forward' are two of his), Gladwell is to cultural commentary what Marshall McLuhan was to communication in the 60s.

Like colleague Surowiecki, he makes his point by anecdote and example: the commercial failure of New Coke a decade ago is put down to a failure of rapid cognition. When tasted blind, consumers notoriously prefer Pepsi. Tasted sighted and poured from a can rather than sipped from a glass, the mysteries of rapid cognition take over and enhance perception of the world's biggest burp. The parallels to wine are obvious and could explain why vinous big names are notoriously shy to enter blind tasting tourneys.

Blink: the Power of Thinking Without Thinking is a handbook for the first two seconds of experience that sets off a sequence of jumps to a series of conclusions. For wine, initial appearance, aroma and taste are worth far more than any amount of swooshing around the mouth and cogitating.

More data is not necessarily more information. Gladwell is the prophet of what he terms 'the power of thin slicing', a strategy at odds with our current cultural paradigm that sees trials last for years, such as that of Milosevic. Whether thin slicing tastings, where each entry is evaluated in two seconds, would yield better results than days of deliberation is an open question. Certainly, the ability to process many more entries would mean boosted profits for show organisers and provide extra fodder for the wine press.

As mentioned earlier, Don Quixote was one of the first public wine pundits. Cervantes's masterpiece, however, like *Bridget Jones's Diary*, is a paean to ridiculous failure. Perhaps the time has come for the Man from La Mancha to make way for the Boys from New York with their 'no wait' tasting and democratic decisions replacing tortuous titanic struggles with vinous windmills.

Or even the girls from Canada, like Natalie MacLean.

BUTT-BRUSH AND BLAHNIKS

The North American experience has a few amusing quirks, as you'd expect.

With the United States the promised land for South African wine exports, useful information on the North American wine retail market is to be found in *Red, White & Drunk All Over* (Bloomsbury, 2007). Written by 'The World's Best Drinks Writer, a Rhodes Scholarship Finalist and Champion Scottish Highland Dancer' and resident of Ottawa, it highlights some intriguing features of the American wine scene.

Such as 'butt-brush – the sales-killing effect of customers bump-ing into each other' – a serious no-no in Manhattan wine retail (but almost impossible to avoid, in my experience, at Sherry-Lehmann Wine & Spirits on Madison Avenue, as the shop is so crammed with first growths, Super Tuscans and Excelsior Cabernet, the marvel-lously juicy Robertson red that Park Avenue dowagers order by the case at $9.99 a bottle).

MacLean comes as a welcome antidote to Robert Parker, James Molesworth and other gurus of the male persuasion. And a lady's opinion is important: the fair sex buy 77 per cent of the wine sold in the United States and drink around 60 per cent of it. MacLean reveals that shopping behaviour is sexually based and takes place in accordance with ecological principles – the men in hunter mode, ducking in and out of a store as quickly as possible, while women are gatherers, lingering to seek advice. Like 'which wine pairs best with pickled boar's feet?'. Answer: perhaps an off-dry Riesling or even a herbal Sauvignon Blanc.

Research by Australian professor Larry Lockshin is quoted that most buyers spend an average of 38 seconds choosing a bottle, a decision based almost entirely on the label. The point is also made that at social gatherings, wine is the only consumable placed on the dinner table in its original packaging.

Wine labels are seen as billboards, telling your guests what you think of them and how much you're prepared to pay. L labels advertise your taste and sophistication (or lack thereof) and she lists three main reasons for buying wine: a search for comfort, nos-talgia and adventure. As for back labels, MacLean damns them as 'about as believable as a Harlequin romance . . . I usually advise people to skip the blurb, or at least not make it an important fac-tor in their decision.'

Gold foil is also a no-no: 'I can smell the marketing plan from across the store. I'm also suspicious when the owner's signature is scrawled on the label: massive ego alert!' So it's probably safe to assume that she is not a subscriber to the Ernie Els newsletter.

Wine is proposed as an example of the long tail purchasing theory advanced by Chris Anderson, editor of *Wired* magazine. Anderson noted that more than half of Amazon.com's online book sales come from outside their list of 130,000 best-sellers. The inference drawn is that 'everyone's taste departs from the mainstream somewhere and the more we explore alternatives, the more we're drawn to them'.

MacLean argues that wine sales have long tails as even the largest wine brands own less than 5 per cent of the market. Certainly not the case for spirits, where a leading brand can easily command a 50 per cent market share, or the light beer market, where the top 10 account for 99 per cent of sales. That said, her argument is contradicted by another long tail – Yellow Tail – which accounts for 35 per cent of all Australian wine exports to America and was the first brand to move more than a million cases a month.

Not all the retail theory is of the armchair variety, with MacLean putting in a 10-hour shift at Discovery Wines in the Big Apple. Advised to wear comfortable shoes, she fronts up in her 'weekend-wear Manolo Blahniks', just like a character from *Sex and the City*. And the conversation overheard in the aisles? 'Is the winemaker single?'

South Africa has no shortage of marketers with mega mojo, with larger than life Nelson Mandela Square restaurateur Alan Pick, of Butcher's Shop & Grill fame, dominating the Johannesburg on-trade market.

SELLING THE MOMENT

The South African experience has a few peculiarities of its own too.

Mr Pick has been called many things in his time and the launch of Vergelegen's flagship Bordeaux blend, V, added a new word to his lexicon of nicknames: oligopsonist (pronounced oli-GOP-suh-nist). From the Greek *oligo* (few, little) and *opsonia* (purchase), it means 'the market condition where a few buyers control the market for a product'.

A week after the South African launch of V, Pick had: 'Cornered the market. [Vergelegen general manager] Don Tooth owed me a case and the six bottles he sent didn't even touch sides. I then made offers to colleagues in the industry. They made an immediate profit and we ended up with 65 cases which we're selling for R800/bottle take away and R1,600 in the restaurant. Don't give me a hard time about the price – I'm not selling wine, I'm selling the moment. If guys have just signed a R100 million deal, R1,600 is neither here nor there.'

From a quality point of view, Pick reckons V is 'as good' as the Ernie Els blend which 'flies out' his restaurant like a golf ball, while his own-label brand, called Pick's Pick, is a big hit, except with Platter's tasters, who perform their dark art sighted. So how embarrassing to rate the Pick's Pick Merlot two-and-a-half stars (translation: good, everyday drinking) when it is *exactly the same wine* as the four-star stunner (translation: excellent) from Jordan Winery.

The one made by Andries Burger at Paul Cluver Estate in Elgin was not so star-crossed, made as it was with Pick's only instruction that it be 'as smooth as possible'. Pick calls it his 'Bryanston option' for people who want to do better than a bottle of Guardian Peak at twice the price.

An interesting twist is the designation of the wine as a product of 'Afrique du Sud', which will ensure it a top left berth on any foreign supermarket shelf, above and to the left of those other New World favourites, Australia and Argentina. Let's hope no one cottons on to Africa Borwa, which is how the majority of South African citizens refer to their mother/fatherland and certainly a lexicographic advance on Azania, which doesn't even beat Austria in the supermarket positioning stakes.

And positioning is the name of the game, with Aussie corporate Southcorp reportedly paying UK supermarket chain Tesco £1 million to secure prime position for its products in end-of-aisle gondolas, a figure set to rise if targets were met. Alas, Christmas sales were lower than expected and Southcorp was asked to take back some of the surplus wine.

While most consumers will agree that R1,000 is a lot of money to pay for a bottle of wine, it is worth mentioning that the 1985 vintage of Sassicaia, the first of the Super Tuscans to secure a perfect Parker pointing, will now set you back £1,000 a bottle according to *How to Spend It*, the glossy monthly insert into the weekend *Financial Times*, the de facto Bible of conspicuous consumption. With all the benefits of hindsight, the first vintages of Sassicaia now look incredibly cheap, a fate Vergelegen marketing manager Eddie Turner earnestly hopes will befall V.

Taking a contrarian view in this high-price hysteria, UK wine scribe Robert Joseph, in town once a year for the Swiss International Wine Awards, reckons that some South African wine 'is too cheap to be taken seriously'. As an example, he quotes the case of Lynx Shiraz made by Dieter Sellmeyer on Lusthof farm in the foothills of the Klein Drakenstein Mountains just outside Franschhoek. With a tiny production of 1,000 cases, Joseph reckons the R80 selling price is way too low. With most of his crop sold to Marc Kent at Boekenhoutskloof (whose Syrah Norman Goodfellow's lists at R268 per bottle), Lynx is 'too cheap to compete'.

With wine prices governed by the laws of supply and demand (at least in the long run), the cornering activities of Pick will at most be a short-lived blip on the retail radar screen. And at the end of the day, Vergelegen should be thankful for these monopolistic manoeuvres which bring free advertising to their product. After all, the farm is owned by the Anglo American Corporation, founded by the Oppenheimers, a family who have some experience in monopolistic trading through their diamond trading company, De Beers.

Selling wine has a lot in common with selling diamonds: they're both activities at the high end of the sex market. Which could explain why so many products behave like fine wine from a marketing point of view.

SHAPESHIFTING

Wine is aspirational so it should come as no surprise to note that other products sometimes try to steal the script.

Fine wine is increasingly becoming the victim of identity theft. Fiji Water, that favourite tipple in *Sex and the City*, is sold on its volcanic terroir, and chocolatier Valrhona is credited with discovering both *goût de terroir* and vintage in chocolates, like its single-plantation Gran Couva from Trinidad. *Wine Spectator* reports the 2001 vintage is 'roasted and rustic tasting, but still plenty fruity'.

And while wine guides find chocolate galore in the Diemersfontein Pinotage and Kevin Arnold's Shiraz, chocolatiers return the compliment, with Maricel Presilla comparing the flavour of the white porcelana cacao bean to 'a fine California Cabernet Sauvignon' in *The New Taste of Chocolate* (Ten Speed Press, 2001). Although philosophers might frown at the circularity of her arguments when Cabernet tastes of chocolate and vice versa.

The latest hedonists to climb on the vintage terroir bandwagon are perfumers like Givenchy with their millésime or vintage editions of VIC (Very Irresistible Givenchy). Fine wine is the victim of a hedonistic hijack by savvy marketers who appropriate all of wine's best lines, the devils.

Like the tag-line of site specificity. Single vineyard wines are flavour of the month in South Africa and perfumers have started cottoning on to the mystique of special sites: *jasminium grandiflorum* from Gowl Bazaar in Tamil Nadu, wild mimosa from Tanneron in the Var and that special orange grove in Nabeul, Tunisia.

The connection between perfume and fine wine was made by Karen Wheeler, writing on 'scent, the new wine' in the *Financial Times*. Calling Château de Beaucastel, however, 'a small wine producer near Avignon' is an understatement of the same quantum as describing Albert Einstein as an egghead or Picasso as a talented interior decorator. But to a beauty writer, the iconic winery of Châteauneuf-du-Pape was merely the venue for a 'tasting' of a new male fragrance from fragrance house Hermès. Called Terre d'Hermès, that it sounds an awful lot like terroir is no accident.

Paméla Roberts, creative director of L'Artisan Parfumeur, told Ms Wheeler that the attraction of the Tunisian orange blossoms was 'A combination of soil and the weather patterns of that particular year . . . at first it smells very green and fresh but then it becomes very sensual, almost animal, and very warm. Every expert who has smelt it is very impressed by it.'

Sounds like winespeak to me.

But perfumers still have a couple of tricks to learn. The admission that differences between vintage and non-vintage flowers 'is a difference in quality of raw materials that professionals can detect, but I'm not sure how noticeable it would be to a normal customer' would not go down well with wine anoraks. And something must have been lost in translation from the www.bulgariatravel. org website which trumpets the use of Bulgarian roses in Helena Rubenstein's Life Pearl creme [sic] along with Indian jasmine and Moroccan Iris concrete.

The appropriation of wine concepts by perfumers is no one-way street. The latest addition to the winespeak vocabulary comes from the heady world of perfumery: sillage. Which may be defined as the olfactory wake left by a person wearing a scent. New Yorker magazine defines it more metaphorically as 'the sense of a person being present in the room after s/he has left'.

A good example of a cuvée with oodles of sillage was the maiden vintage Nouvelle (a crossing of Sémillon and Crouchen Blanc by Chris Orffer) from Boland Cellars, which has olfactory and flavour characteristics reminiscent of Sauvignon Blanc and Viognier.

The only drawback is that the term is French, an advantage for pompous pundits, but a drawback for everyone else. A translation is fraught with danger: dropping an 'l' refers to fodder obtained by fermenting green forage plants in a silo – perhaps of some use in a Sauvignon Blanc tasting. Adding a 'u', one gets suillage, which ends up in a drain, while swapping an 'i' for a 'u' gives *sullage*, a synonym for sewage, which would liven up the 'also tasted' category of panel tastings no end.

COUTURE AND CUVÉES

Fine wine is a powerful fashion accessory.

Wine reportage is on the move: out of the lifestyle supplements and onto the business pages. Like the pink ones of the *Financial Times*, the most authoritative business broadsheet of them all. 'Bordeaux Toasts 2005 Vintage', screamed the headline, with the news that 'demand for the exceptional 2005 vintage is likely to smash pricing records and leave many enthusiasts floundering to secure cases of wine'.

I read the story on a TAP flight from Lisbon to Maputo, shortly after I'd broken my own record for wine spend: €150 on a bottle of Charme '02 made by Dirk van der Niepoort in the Douro. It had been that or a choice of two vintages of Portugal's icon wine, Barca Velha, at the same price. The venue was the Binhoteca wine bar in Sintra and manager Nino Santos rated the Charme way above the old boat. The caliphs who used to run Sintra must have been spinning in their kramats, just like my bank manager when the credit card bill came home to roost.

But €150 in a wine bar for Portugal's finest red is small potatoes compared to 2005 Bordeaux you buy now for release in a couple of years' time. First growth Château Haut Brion, a favourite tipple of seventeenth-century diarist Samuel Pepys, is on offer to *négociants* at €240 a bottle *en primeur*. This first step in a convoluted delivery chain will pass it on to merchants, who will sell it to retailers, who will ship it to collectors, with everyone making a tidy profit along the way. Of course the stuff is unlikely to ever be drunk – it's simply too valuable.

Berry Bros. & Rudd, the London wine merchant in up-market

St. James's, reckons a case of 12 bottles of Château Latour and its ilk will set you back £4,000 – over triple the price of my Charme before any on-consumption markup. Good news for Latour proprietor and French supermarket supremo François Pinault, who also owns Gucci. Which is the real story in the whole greedy affair: fine wine has become a fashion accessory to be marketed to status-conscious new wealth in emerging markets.

And that neatly explains the label on my Charme: a tailor's mannequin outlined in pattern stitch. A far simpler one than my first guess, which had tailor morphing into Taylor, one of the oldest and grandest port houses and competitor to Niepoort, which is all far too Jacques Derrida for a single bottle of red.

But the point is easily made: fashionistas are the new winos, and that Bernard Arnault owns both Louis Vuitton and Château Cheval Blanc is no accident. Grande Marque bubbly cottoned on to the similarities between couture and champagne some time ago, with the neoprene sleeve for La Grande Dame '96 from Veuve Clicquot just one example. Closer to home, the Nederburg fashion show was always the highlight of the annual wine auction and vice versa, with the brand a headline sponsor for Cape Town Fashion Week.

Back with larger than life ladies, *Decanter* reported that the *grande dame* of Bordeaux, octogenarian May-Eliane de Lencquesaing, was involved in discussions with French fashion house Hèrmes to sell a major stake in one of the golden geese of Bordeaux (and neighbour to Château Latour), second growth Château Pichon Longueville Comtesse de Lalande – or to form an alliance, as it is more euphemistically put. Louis Roederer eventually gobbled it up (or should that be slurped it down?), but Hèrmes was most definitely in the frame for a while.

A view of the glossy future of fine wine comes free with *How to Spend It*, a monthly supplement of the *Financial Times*. Edited by Gillian de Bono (I'm still trying to think of a lateral thinking trick to find out if she's related to Edward), it 'lifts the lid on the high life, deconstructs style icons, debunks dotcoms and provides secret remedies for those affected by galloping consumption', as you do during a flight to Maputo.

Lucia van der Post is a frequent contributor and her late dad, Sir Laurens, that well-known fibber and fantasist, is frequently mentioned in the periodic polls to determine the top 100 South Africans.

A random dissection gives a completely non-scientific inventory of today's lifestyle issues and concerns. What's hot and what's not. Travel gets five pages – including two for Biarritz, two for the French Riviera (both handy Easyjet destinations, with founder Stelios Haji-Ioannou awarded that ultimate fashion accessory, a knighthood, in June). Fine art and interior design get three each; celebrity chat and yachting get a couple, while techie, glamour and jewellery gadgets each get a page. The winner by far, however, is fashion, with eight.

In the sweaty grip of a northern hemisphere summer, Van der Post advocates spending on fashion accessories: 'New accessories are even more important than new outfits.' Which reinforces the seasonal nature of haute couture, where new outfits are like vintages, you need a new one every season. For South African consumers living upside down vis-à-vis the Europeans, what to drink in winter is a no-brainer, with new vintages for tasting at wine festivals, which in format and function are just like fashion shows, complete with divas, over-the-top creations, anoraks in bow ties and celebrities galore.

As fashion accessories go, gloves, belts, bags and even fur (Gucci's velvet evening shoes are a snip at R5,000 complete with mink-embellished straps) are in, while for summery Sauvignon Blanc, South Africa proposes two options: the first is tropical and fruity, from traditionally warmer areas like Stellenbosch, Paarl and across the mountains in Robertson and Worcester. (Although that said, Springfield makes a true Kiwi *doppelgänger* through judicious harvesting and the services of a reverse osmosis machine.)

Sauvignon Blanc Type II comes from the west coast, from Elgin

down south to Elim, with a racy, grassier character of steely goose-
berry and grapefruit. First Sighting, which commemorates Bar-
tholomeu Dias and his 15th-century voyage of discovery around
the Cape, is a good example. For those with exotic tastes, Viognier
is as OTT as anything by Alessandro dell'Acqua, while a well-
wooded Chardonnay is the wine world's version of Coco Chanel's
little black dress.

It's no surprise to note that France and northern Italy are the
home of haute couture: they provide the same service for fine wine.
The pursuit of excellence using best quality ingredients is a common mission statement for both Alsace and Armani, for Bordeaux
and Balenciaga (their wedge biker boot in camel skin rings in at
£1,085).

While high-profile designers like Christian Lacroix and Jean Paul
Gaultier may be as irresistibly romantic as *garagiste* producers like
the Black Pearl Winery and the Foundry, in both activities, brands
play a vital role. Manolo Blahnik jewelled stilettos may look great,
but I'm told they're hell on the back in the same way that more
than a bottle of Le Pin overloads both palate and wallet. While
icons are great for special occasions, it's Boschendal and Benetton
for everyday consumption.

The secret of looking good and drinking well is coordination.
'Last year's shoes, an ill-judged bag, a dated hairstyle and you
might as well have saved the dosh,' according to La Lucia. Red
blends are a bit like that. Take a tight and elegant Cabernet Franc
and add a jammy Merlot and you don't need Mr Micawber to tell
you the answer.

Celebrity culture certainly has an effect. WOSA spends part of
its annual R27 million budget on promotional videos, and on the
visual evidence of the last one, South African wine is all made by
photogenic twenty- and thirty-something metrosexual males in
the same way the hottest fashions are made by Stella McCartney
(b.1972) and Alexander McQueen (b.1969).

Although with *garagiste* Syrah on sale in South African restaurants for several hundred rand a bottle *more* than Rhône benchmarks like La Chapelle, hasn't the celebrity pendulum swung too far? There are certainly rumours of a style change: the excesses of previous seasons (too high alcohol levels and overripe fruit, big hairdos and shoulder pads) are all being toned down. As US *Vogue* puts it, 'there's a new gal in town and she makes sobriety look utterly sexy'.

But perhaps the strangest thing about wine and fashion is the return of the unfashionable: fur and Pinotage are presently both making like boomerangs. On which subject, Lucia van der Post again: 'There is nothing to beat a fur shrug or stole for adding instant *jolie madame* to any outfit.' Cape winemakers are finding the same thing with Pinotage in a blend – just ask Danie Steytler, whose Vision '01 was best blend at the International Wine and Spirit Competition in London, that well-known capital of wine and fashion.

SIGN LANGUAGE

I had the good fortune to dine with the creator of that bottle of Charme '02 in 2008.

'You speak to me
In sign language
As I'm eating a sandwich
In a small cafe
At a quarter to three.'

(BOB DYLAN, *Sign Language*)

OK, so the sandwich was foie gras on melba toast and the small café was Harald Bresselschmidt's award-winning Aubergine res-taurant in Gardens and we were out by 1 (am), but Dirk van der Niepoort's response to what his family thought of his first dry red table wines was a sign language classic – a corkscrew motion of his index finger against his temple (translation: crazy).

For the fifth generation of a port-producing family to throw away the *aguardente* and make an unfortified table wine is a bit like Ronald McDonald's son announcing he's become vegetarian. Which is exactly what Niepoort did back in 1990. With the business now evenly split between fortified ports and table wine, he did have the grace to admit the 2005 Niepoort vintage port is the best wine he has ever made. ('Serious shit', as he put it.)

'It's unbalanced vineyards that make a truly great port,' he continued, 'but you need balanced vineyards to make great wine.' Niepoort speaks with the self-confidence of the self-taught. Having studied economics in Switzerland, he's happy he didn't study winemaking at a university: 'I haven't been castrated. I went on a course at [University of California at] Davis once. It was on filtration and was sponsored by the filtering companies. After hearing them tell it, I was imagining giant monsters in my wine if I didn't filter.' Then out with the index finger and that corkscrew motion again.

Niepoort is refreshingly iconoclastic: national grape Touriga Naçional 'is a disaster for Portugal. Everyone is planting it and soon all our wines will taste the same.' His first trip to South Africa was in 2007 when he hired a camper van and toured the Western Cape with his family. He fell in love with South Africa, he admits, but has some surprising observations.

'Calitzdorp [the port capital of South Africa] was a big disappointment. Just because it's hot, doesn't mean it's automatically suitable for port. Everything was wrong. We drove through much better terroir on the way there.' An offhand comment that evoked a furious letter to the editor of *WINE* from Carl Nel, owner of Boplaas. Putting his money where his mouth is, Niepoort is now making a port-style wine with local winemaking phenomenon Eben Sadie. A blend of Syrah, Pinotage and Tinta Barocca, it will obviously not be a traditional port.

Of Sadie's own wines, Niepoort likes them very much but thinks he harvests 'a little bit too late. But then I don't like over-ripe grapes', which is clear from his quartet of fresh reds with high acids. The twin peaks are called Charme, 'heaven for burgundy lovers', and Batuta, made in a more extractive style.

Redoma was the name chosen for his first dry red and it remains his attempt at bottling the hard, mineral character of the Douro, an area so extreme he refuses to illustrate his many talks at wine dinners and anorak jamborees with a Powerpoint slide show. 'Photographs cannot capture the nature of the landscape,' he says. Much better to let your tastebuds do the tourism – oral sign language, if you like.

Comtesse Alexia and the death of South African Chenin

Chenin Blanc is the most widely planted grape varietal in South Africa. It also stirs up the most passion.

When the Bolsheviks shot the Russian royal family in that dark and dirty cellar outside the Siberian *dorp* of Yekaterinburg, conspiracy theorists maintained the reds fired so many bullets that at least one Romanov slipped away in the cloud of gun smoke – the Grand Duchess Anastasia Nikolaevna being the usual suspect. It seems likely she did, as she was last encountered squatting on a yacht in the Cape Town waterfront marina. I bumped into her at the cocktail party launch of Woolworth's Comtesse Alexia Brut Champagne held at One.Waterfront, the restaurant at the Cape Grace Hotel that gave celebrity chef Bruce Robertson his first shot at fame and was still listing him as an attraction several years after he left.

Now a bag lady (literally, as her blue Pick 'n Pay shopping tote drew attention at the Woolies do), the Grand Duchess was on her way to borrow an envelope from the hotel reception to smarten up her US visa application, when a waiter thrust a glass of bubbly into her hand and directed her to the party. Her adopted yacht was en route to Miami by way of Brazil and the days of royal *laissez-passer* being long past, she thought she'd stand more chance being hired as crew if her paperwork was in order. 'I'm a grotty yachtie,' she announced merrily as she knocked back the bubbles. 'Is there anything to eat? I'm famished. I haven't eaten for two days.'

Fortified with some foie gras parfait and a couple of spring rolls with sweet chilli dip, the Duchess defended the Pick 'n Pay bag she was slipping her cheese course into. 'I got it at a Checker's function,'

she explained with a laugh. Brown eyes swimming alarmingly
behind bottle top spectacles, it must have seemed like the old days
back in the St Petersburg palace watching papa play with his bejew-
elled Fabergé eggs, although the Comtesse Alexia champagne must
have tasted much drier than the fizz she and sister, Olga, had been
accustomed to. Brut (ie extra dry), with a residual sugar content of
10 g/l, it was a racy contrast to the 50 g/l demi-sec style preferred at
the Russian court. So much so in fact that the style was nicknamed
goût russe, with brut the *goût anglais* while the dry style in between
was known in the trade as the *goût américain*.

After several years of global economic boom, conspicuous consumption is now firmly back in fashion. So it makes total sense for
a supermarket to be African pioneers of an own-brand champagne,
to be loaded into the trolley along with a pack of eco-friendly toilet
rolls, organic snopeas and Fairtrade coffee. The term conspicuous
consumption was coined at the end of the nineteenth century in the
so-called 'gilded age' before World War I to describe the lifestyle of
the Vanderbilts and Rockefellers. Whole blocks of Manhattan were
taken up with their mansions and fabulous art treasures of Renaissance Europe were emigrating across the Atlantic at a frightening
rate of knots. There seemed to be no bottom to these Yankee pockets. At his richest, John D. Rockefeller earned 2 per cent of America's GDP – on that measure the world's wealthiest individual today,
Bill Gates, at a measly 0.5 per cent, has some way to go.

But perhaps the most conspicuous consumers of that gilded
period were the Romanovs before the October Revolution (which,
perversely, actually took place in November 1918). Pre-revolution-
ary Moscow was the main market for French luxury exports, from
Impressionist paintings to grande marque champagne. So when the
First World War descended over the continent, the imperial army,
commanded by a cast of thousands straight out of Tolstoy's *War
and Peace*, insisted on their home comforts. Even in the far reaches
of the Russian empire, such as the garrison in Finland.

Which explains the cargo of a military supply ship, the wooden

ketch *Jonkoping*: 3,500 bottles of vintage (1907) Heidsieck Monopole champagne and enough cognac in cask to fill 80,000 bottles
– presumably for all those long winter nights. However, she was
sunk by a German U-boat in 1916 – and that's where the treasure
lay, perfectly preserved for over 80 years in the cold and dark waters
of the Baltic, until raised by intrepid Danish salvers.

Which surely scores bonus points for effort among the pluto-
crats and share option beneficiaries who can now pay R30,000 at
branches of Caviar House in London for their own bottle of *goût
russe*. For those with champagne taste and supermarket budgets,
Comtesse Alexia is a lot cheaper at R195 a bottle, and more widely
available. Just how far conspicuous consumption has trickled down
the South African financial snakes and ladders board is clear when
you are told that Woolies are the largest South African retailers of
that favourite tipple of the Romanovs, Veuve Clicquot. It sells for
R335 a bottle and buyer Ivan Oertle reports the Alexia pre-orders
are larger than those for Veuve.

Which is probably just as well, as the Alexia overdelivers by at
least R100 a bottle. Not that you have to pay for your drinks at the
widow's house in Reims, the Hotel de Marc complete with bul-
let holes from a domestic with some neighbours across the Rhine.
Here, the white-gloved sommelier still decants the demi-sec into a
crystal decanter before serving. Tastefully transformed into a corporate hospitality pit stop, rooms in the Château feature ball–and–
claw baths standing in splendid isolation in marble bathrooms and
bar fridges stocked with product humming quietly in the corner.
Does anyone ever take advantage? Most visitors open one bottle
at the most, except for South African politicians and Russian oli-
garchs, who clean out the fridge into their Louis Vuitton bags. Quite
what the South Africans do next is debatable, with liquids no longer admissible in airline hand luggage. Sorry, I forgot. They have
their own gravy planes.

The Grand Duchess was suitably vague as to whether we could
come back to the yacht for a look around, muttering something

about having some cleaning to do, as they planned to set sail on Sunday, so thoughts turned to dinner for the dregs of the launch party. With George Jardine's Bree Street restaurant so full not even a call from 'kitchen cowboy,' Pete Goffe-Wood could winkle out a place, the dregs decided to move on to Belthazar, taking three bottles of Comtesse Alexia along for company.

Pete's wife Elize secured a table from Cape Town's most urbane maitre d', Jonathan Steyn (UK designer Paul Smith was simultaneously opening a shop on the Waterfront with Taittinger on tap, which explained why the queue for tables was only in double digits). Steyn exchanged a bottle of Capaia 2004 for an Alexia. 'It's an emotional wine for me,' he explained, 'being the last vintage made by Tibor Gàl before he died in a car crash.' Although it was emotion of a different sort that passed briefly across his face as the kitchen cowboy sent his rare rump back for the second time ('it's worse than the first one – too cold', he pronounced, index finger pushed accusingly into the bloody flesh as if being directed by Quentin Tarantino).

Gàl was one of the heroes of modern wine, being the man responsible for the best vintages of Ornellaia. He died when his car came off second best to a bus. Gàl had been dining with his boss, Baron Alexander von Essen, who was obliquely responsible for the development of champagne-style wines in South Africa.

A famous hunter of exotic beasts, Von Essen belonged to the same exclusive hunting club as the Kentucky neighbour of coal magnate Graham Beck. Beck is the master of the default business model. In the 80s, he had helped a bankrupt farmer friend out in Robertson and now owned a horse farm on the wrong side of the mountain. A great place to make champagne, advised Von Essen, who introduced Beck to Jan Boland Coetzee as the rainmaker required to make it happen. Coetzee recommended Achim von Arnim's apprentice, Pieter Ferreira, for the job of winemaker and the rest is history.

Back at Belthazar, hardly had the rare Chicago cut with whole grain mustard on the side disappeared down the cakehole, than *WINE* magazine deputy editor (since promoted to the editor's La-Z-Boy recliner) Christian Eedes appeared at the table brandishing a bottle of 2001 Teddy Hall Chenin Blanc like Banquo's ghost at Macbeth's last dinner party. 'Our Chenin Challenge is dead,' he wailed, referring to his organ's Chenin competition. 'It's the end of world-class wines like this.' It was certainly the end of something, including the *WINE* Christmas lunch at Buitenverwachting that had overrun and become a R1,200 dinner for four at Belthazar, including managing editor Michael Froud.

Images of Banquo's babies being thrown out with the bathwater swam into my consciousness. Was the impending death of South African Chenin all my fault? Was a story I penned for the *Financial Mail* instrumental in supermarket chain Spar cancelling its R175,000 annual sponsorship of the Chenin Challenge? The issue was one of principle.

In the 2006 Challenge, chairman of judges Michael Fridjhon, whose Reciprocal Wine Trading Company imports some of the finest French Chenin, had instructed his fellow pundits 'to be on our guard against being seduced by sugar', but at the same time urged the panel not to reward wines that showed 'elegance without substance'. The first part of the instruction was guaranteed to be controversial, given that the previous Challenge winner was Teddy Hall's Rudera Robusto 2002, a wine with 15.7 g/l of residual sugar. As the late high priestess of soul, Nina Simone, remarked, 'I want a little sugar in my bowl/I want a little sweetness down in my soul.'

Visions of Spar executives hurrying down from the balmy sugarcane fields of Pinetown KZN for an emergency *bosberaad* with the Pinelands pundits of *WINE* flashed through my mind. The charges of panel–prodding by a chairman who in any case consults to a competing supermarket chain were rejected by the publisher who, like Tammy Wynette, gallantly stood by his man. Exit Spar sponsorship. The explanation offered for the change of sponsor in the *Sunday Times* ('having expensive wines winning the award was embarrassing, as Spar franchise holders had problems moving the winning stock') rang hollow when it was the keenly priced Spier 2004 Chenin which won the last Challenge.

But was it even sweetness or an attempt to keep Teddy's expensive tipples out of the medals that prompted the sugar fatwa? Certainly, a preference for drier styles flies in the face of current tastes. Some commentators call high residual sugar (RS) the single factor that makes Australian Yellow Tail the most successful wine in the world. In the all-important (for South African exporters) UK market, rosé wines are on a roll, with market share up from 2.7 per cent in 2000 to 7 per cent in 2006. This rosé renaissance is largely a US-driven initiative, with six million cases being sold under the Blossom Hill and Gallo brands. Most of the time, RS exceeds 15 g/l with total acidity also proportionally higher in these wines.

With the aim of the competition to stimulate Chenin sales, surely a popular style should override aesthetic prejudices of the minority? Especially in a competition sponsored by a supermarket chain.

Chenin king Teddy Hall is not afraid of RS. He comments: 'Sauvignon Blanc and Chardonnay can taste cheap and nasty with some RS, but Chenin Blanc and (Rhine) Riesling sometimes need some residual sugar for balance.' Although he's not too worried about the instruction to judges, as while it may penalise his Robusto (running to anything between 10 and 20 g/l RS), it should aid his Rudera (between 3.5 and 5.5 g/l RS). 'Winning is a lottery anyway,' he continues, 'and I don't make wines for competitions, although it's always nice to win them. By the way, it is interesting to note that Chenin Blanc and (Rhine) Riesling are the longest living white wines in the world, with and without high RS.'

This aversion to sweetness by show judges is nothing new. Judging the inaugural Diners Club Young Winemaker of the Year Award with a catch-all category of white wine, there was much consternation when a noble late harvest topped the poll and an attempt to replace the winner was only headed off by two judges digging in their heels.

Which confirms a problem with blind-tasting panels highlighted in a letter to the editor of *WINE*. In discussions after individual blind assessments, 'a dominant personality or more experienced adjudicator could sway the majority of the forum into a collective score that may not be accurate', which, in my experience, happens all the time.

Of course, this problem does not arise in sighted tastings, as the prejudices of individual tasters are fully reflected in their assessments to start with. Which all rather marginalises competitions and wine guides when the public has different criteria and preferences to judges.

All food for thought for South African winemakers who make the stuff to sell it rather than win competitions. At the end of the day, the consumer's palate is king. As Ms Simone concluded: 'Maybe I can fix things up so they'll go/whatsa matter daddy/come on save my soul/drop a little sugar in my bowl.'

After Spar withdrew its sponsorship shilling, First National Bank Private Clients – a true mouthful with or without RS – gallantly stepped into the breach and funded the even more controversial 2007 Chenin Challenge. The winner was a 2004 Val du Chêne from KWV, quickly dubbed 'Val du Shame' by the industry when it emerged that Ian Nieuwoudt, later dismissed for adding flavourants to Laborie Sauvignon Blanc, was white winemaker in charge at the time.

When I excused myself from the slap-up awards lunch at Etienne Bonthuys's award-winning Tokara restaurant to phone Ian my congratulations, he told me, somewhat ominously, I thought at the time, 'You don't know how happy I am that that particular wine won.'

While question marks continue to fly at the chemical nature of the winning wine, exhibit B on the Death of Chenin's charge sheet was how the 'Shame' laid claim to the prize.

Five judges scored eight finalist wines blind out of 20 with Ken Forrester's FMC 2004 ending up with a combined tally two points ahead of the Shame, or almost half a point per judge, a significant difference as wine quality scales are notoriously non-linear.

When the anomaly of the winning wine scoring over 2 per cent less than the runner-up was pointed out, the explanation offered was that the scores of the two top wines were so close it was decided to rank the top eight, with two judges choosing the Shame and the other three each choosing a different wine. (For mathematical proof of why this is the kind of result you'd expect if the judges were a troop of teetotal monkeys, see the Appendix.)

It was quickly leaked that FMC winemaker and judge Martin Meinert had voted for the Shame, in effect giving it victory by behaving like a gentleman. The FMC, being far higher in alcohol and residual sugar than the other finalists, must have been easy to recognise and being of the old school, Meinert presumably thought it bad form to vote for his own wine, thereby leaving the door open for the Shame to slip through.

Of course, Meinert's vote should never have been included in the first place, in which case the remaining four judges each voted for a different wine, with thus four winners and the idea that there was one (or even two) superior styles of South African Chenin in the spittoon along with the expectorated crumbs of cream cracker. Whichever way you cut and dice it, the result looks like a fix and that's even discounting the widespread rumours and forwarded SMSs of undeclared consultancies between judges and contestants.

The (almost) final word must go to the public via tastings of Chenin Challenge finalists in Johannesburg and Cape Town (a nice little earner for WINE, with punters paying R100 a ticket to taste competition wine). The FMC 2004 was firm favourite (with the Mulderbosch barrel-fermented Chenin '06 – wittily called Steen op Hout – also making many friends), aided in no small measure by the star appeal of winemaker and tasting co-presenter Michael Dobrovic. The Shame underwhelmed, suffering from 'huge bottle variation', although one winemaker did compliment it on a remarkable and persistent guava character, inadvertently feeding the added flavourant fire.

Indeed, when Pete Goffe-Wood and the *Cape Times's* dapper wine pundit, J. P. Rossouw, put the winning Chenin through its paces at Aubergine restaurant in Cape Town for a Chef's Challenge feature for *WINE*, Aubergine chef Harald Bresselschmidt said he found it difficult to match the Shame with any dish as the wine lacked structure. An observation with which Rossouw and Goffe-Wood concurred.

When I eventually tracked down a bottle to Marc's Mediterranean Cuisine and Garden Restaurant in Paarl (reasonably priced at R100) with Bernd Philippi, Bernd dismissed it as boring. We abandoned half the bottle and moved on to a much more exciting Thelema Sutherland Sauvignon Blanc.

RUMINATIONS ON RUMI

After some serious gastric reflux brought on by such a shameful tale, some ruminations on Rumi are called for.

Michael Dobrovic was assured of his place on *WINE*'s Chenin roadshow, as he is widely regarded as one of the most gifted winemakers in South Africa. His barrel-fermented Chardonnay is a regular feature of *Wine Spectator's* Top 100 Wines of the Year. One reason for this could be that he is in tune with America's psyche thanks to a passion for the poetry of a Persian mystic, Rumi. Which in itself is something of a curiosity.

The gulf between the Islamic republic of Iran and the United States has never loomed larger, yet there are similarities between the two countries: both are theocratic republics run by religious fundamentalists and they share the most popular poet: Jalal al-Din Rumi, a 13th-century whirling dervish, mystical Sufi bard who achieved transcendence through dancing. His popularity in Iran is a no-brainer, where his ecstatic poetry is considered second only to the Qu'ran. With a hardliner now in power, Rumi's appeal will be enhanced, as mysticism flourishes under doctrinal pressure.

Over in the Great Satan, a professor of English from Tennessee, Coleman Barks, has done for Rumi what Edward Fitzgerald did for Omar Khayyám with an entertaining translation of Rumi's 25,000 spiritual couplets called *Masnavi-ye Ma'navi*. According to *The Guardian*, the *oeuvre* deals with: 'Taverns and tattoo parlours, demons and talking trees and dugongs that graze on hyacinth beds. They are both worldly and otherworldly.' No wonder he is the favourite bard of celebrities such as Madonna, Goldie Hawn, composer Philip Glass and the queen of New York's fashionistas, Donna Karan.

Born Muhammad al-Balkhi in 1207 in what is now Tajikistan, he acquired the name Rumi from his long residence in the city of Rum in the heart of the Byzantine Empire. In 1244, his life changed when he ran off with an ageing mystic called Shams of Tabriz who taught him how to attain religious ecstasy by whirling to the music of a grass lute.

In 1247, the picture becomes a little unclear. Some authorities simply say that Shams disappeared. Others claim he was killed by Ala'uddin, Rumi's jealous second son. Whatever the facts, Rumi searched for his friend without results, describing it as the search for his own identity: 'Indeed I sought my own self, that is sure, fermenting in the vat, just like the must.' After the loss of his friend, Rumi turned to poetry for consolation.

Rumi called himself a man created from the wine of love and for him drunkenness was part of the mystical whole, a glimpse of the possibility of ecstatic intoxication. Many of his poems deal with wine and have a timeless message that still resonates today. Like his advice to exhibitors at WineX on a Friday night: 'If you pour an entire jar filled with joyous wine on the head of those already drunk, what do you think will happen?' Or for Platter's tasters: 'You only need smell the wine for vision to flame from each void – such flames from wine's aroma! Imagine if you were the wine.'

Encouragement for entrants to the Diners Club Winelist of the Year Award: 'When the host of the tavern became my heart-mate, my blood turned to wine and my heart to kebab. When the eye is filled with thought of him, a voice arrives: well done, O flagon, and bravo, wine!' And one in praise of bottle maturation: 'When grapes combine their juice and are closed up together for a time in a dark place, the results are spectacular.'

The ecstatic ruminations of Rumi stand in stark contrast to the rampant commercialism that attempts to hijack wine for its own ends. As film-maker Jonathan Nossiter summed it up after making *Mondovino*: 'It's an industry that is based on greed, profit, the infantilization of tastes, in which stupidity is covered up by special effects . . . ' For Rumi, wine is much more than this. It's a metaphor for life itself: 'In the tavern are many wines – the wine of delight in color and form and taste, the wine of the intellect's agility, the fine port of stories, and the cabernet of soul singing.'

While the now sponsorless Chenin Challenge has generated a lot of heat, sound and more than a few column centimetres, whether the future of South Africa's most planted cultivar rests in its gift is a bit of a stretch. Indeed, when *The New York Times* reviewed South African Chenin two months after the Challenge, not one of the 2007 finalists made it into the line-up of 25 wines they tasted.

THE NEW YORK TIMES WEIGHS IN

While WOSA may advise South African producers to concentrate on Europe for export sales, Noo Yawkers have a thing for South African Chenin.

Is *The New York Times* wine writer, Eric Asimov, related to the famous Brooklyn claustrophile and sci-fi scribbler, Isaac Asimov, author or editor of more than 500 books (my favourite: *Azazel, the Two Centimeter Demon*)? Asimov died of AIDS in 1992, contracted from a blood transfusion.

On the one hand, Isaac's first sci-fi story was called *Cosmic Cork-screw* and his theme of paternalism (the first robot book, *Robbie,* featured a robotic nanny) would suit the patriarch of a winespeak dynasty. On the other, Eric doesn't seem to be very up to date for a writer with futuristic genes, as Waterford winemaker François Haasbroek reported in a letter to the *Grape* blog www.grape.org.za.

Surfing the web, Haasbroek discovered that *The New York Times's* own wine blog, *Pour*, run by Eric, had links to websites providing information on South Africa that was spectacularly out of date. François' favourite was the assertion that 'KWV actually still controls price, supply and demand of grapes', although perhaps information on the 'Analusia appellation' showed some extraterrestrial connections.

Certainly, Eric is prone to flights of fancy. In his feature on South African Chenin Blanc, he noted: 'The prime South African wine region, which arches around Cape Town at the southern confluence of the Atlantic and Indian oceans, might be theoretically too warm and humid for making fine wines.' A statement immediately contradicted by the image of a vineyard with the caption: 'South Africa's cool climate and low rainfall favour the grapes at a vineyard near Cape Town.'

This geographic confusion is shared with another wine writing Manhattan sipper, Jay McInerney, who notes in *A Hedonist in the Cellar* that the vineyards of his friend, ace nightclub dancer Anthony Hamilton Russell are located 'less than two miles from the Indian Ocean', confirming the American cliché of terminally confused geography.

Pedantic quibbles aside, what is interesting is the *Times's* selection of the best South African Chenin available in the Big Apple. Twenty-five wines were sampled and six are featured – with not a single 2007 Chenin Challenge finalist among them.

So there's clearly work to be done on Chenin selection in the United States and one would have thought the FNB Private Clients *WINE* Magazine Chenin Blanc Challenge is the vehicle to achieve that. Blowing its own trumpet in *WINE*, the competition states: 'It is not immodest to claim that the FPCWMCBC, now in its 12th year and with a new co-sponsor in FPC, has played a significant role in facilitating the renaissance of the variety in South Africa.' But perhaps not in the rest of the cosmos.

For of the six wines featured by Asimov, five didn't even enter the Challenge. Spier submitted their Private Collection to the Challenge, while Asimov preferred the Discover Steen (after the Shame won the Challenge, Spier reportedly wished they'd entered their entry-level Discover wine). The unwooded Raats Chenin entered for the FPCWMCBC was the 2006 vintage, while Asimov rated the 2005 top of the *Times* tasting – the vintage difference being perhaps unavoidable given the logistics of shipping wine between continents. Alex Dale is a self-confessed 'wine producer who steers clear of all and any wine competitions', which explains the absence of Vinum from the FPCWMCBC roll of honour.

Haasbroek's own Pecan Stream was not entered for the Challenge, ditto André Shearer's Indaba, for pretty much the same reason as the Discover Steen. 'A first place in the Chenin Challenge or a Platter's five-star accolade has zero marketing value in the United States,' notes Shearer. 'Even if *Decanter* magazine rated our Indaba as best-value Chenin in the world, it would still have no effect in the States,' he added. By way of contrast, Shearer describes an excited Bruwer Raats as being over the moon with sudden international interest in his Chenin in the wake of *The New York Times* story.

Which all depressingly confirms the power of brand *NYT*. Even if some of the facts are sus, some of the wines are second labels and the writer may or may not be an extraterrestrial, a passing mention in that august organ is sufficient to set the phones ringing and the order book bulging.

While the *New York Times* may have ignored the Challenge, one Chenin style yet to be contaminated by the pandemic of dodgy wine shows that have decimated Cape vineyards is sherry. Monis released a fino sherry a couple of months after the 'Shameful' fiasco and Pete the Kitchen Cowboy featured once again. The launch vehicle was a tapas seafood lunch designed by him and held at Salt restaurant in Bantry Bay where you can stare out of the plate glass windows at the ocean rollers all the way to Brazil.

Made from Stellenbosch Chenin fermented for three years under a layer of *flôr* yeast in 60-year-old 500-litre barrels, the wine is remarkable for three reasons: intense nutty flavours; reasonable price (retailing at R45 in an elegant imported 500 ml bottle) and scarcity (14,000 litre total production), most of which was consumed at the lunch, which ended at 7 pm when evening diners got tired of waiting for their tables and demanded evictions.

Six hours earlier, a bottle was dispatched to the table of Finance Minister Trevor Manuel. Dining *à deux*, Trevor was so impressed, he promised to hold liquor tax at current levels. Well, that was what the Maître d' said, but I could have misheard as Monis winemaker Dirkie Christowitz was recounting anecdotes from his dinner at the Castle with Mikhail Kalashnikov (of AK47 fame and intellectual descendant of those Bolshevik shooters in the cellar), a guest of the South African Army general staff.

Whether the Grand Duchess crashed that dinner too is unclear, as she had a waitress job at Topsy Venter's Franschhoek restaurant at the time. Although, like all things in life, that didn't last either, thanks to her habit of laying down her order pad and joining the diners at their meal.

The last word

'*Bronze is the mirror of the outward form*
Wine is the mirror of the mind.'

(AESCHYLUS, 6th century BCE)

The struggle between amateurs and elites for the soul of wine is nothing new. In classical times the two different approaches were adopted by the ancient Greeks and Romans. Terroir started with the Greeks when the drachma dropped that the taste of wine depended on the place the grapes were grown. Different styles of wine were stored in amphorae of different shapes, closed with cork stoppers – a technical innovation later lost and rediscovered again only relatively recently, in the 16th century.

Archestratus, a Greek gourmet living in Sicily, preferred the wines of Lesbos, while others favoured the wines of Thásos and Chios, according to Tom Standage in his *A History of the World in Six Glasses* (Atlantic, 2007). While style was a question of geography, everyone agreed that aged wines were to be preferred to current vintages.

Wine would typically be drunk at a symposium, a social gathering where all would drink from a communal *krater*, diluted with water as only Dionysus and barbarians drank the stuff neat. As Plato noted disapprovingly: 'The Scythians and Thracians, both men and women, drink unmixed wine, which they pour on their garments, and this they think a glorious and happy institution.'

Democratic drinking didn't last long once the Romans got hold of it. The Greek symposium became a Roman convivium where different wines would be served according to one's position in society: Falernian for the top table, then perhaps *mulsum* – a mixture of wine and honey – for the next rank and *rosatum*, wine flavoured with roses – a literal rosé – for the ladies. Soldiers got *posca*, a mixture of water and sour wine, while slaves got *lora,* rehydrated pressings.

The Romans used wine to emphasise social divisions rather than as an exercise in democracy, that crazy Greek idea. Richard Nixon must have been a reincarnated Roman Emperor. On the presidential yacht USS *Sequoia,* he would serve Mouton Cadet to his guests while his butler poured him Château Margaux 1966, artfully wrapped in a towel.

So much for the superiority of Californian wines at the tables of power, a point being made at the 1976 Judgment of Paris tasting, held to commemorate the American bicentenary, at which Californian reds demolished first growths like Margaux in a blind tasting with French judges presiding.

It was the Romans who first swapped Mammon for Bacchus and things got so bad, the Roman Senate passed sumptuary laws as all the conspicuous consumption of food and wine was making the poor restless. Dining rooms had to have windows facing outwards, so inspectors could check on infringements.

With the news confirmed that Gauteng MEC for finance Paul Mashatile followed up his infamous R96,375 lunch at Auberge Michel in 2006 with a meal for R108,229, all charged to Gauteng taxpayers, some form of sumptuary control over Gauteng civil servants is clearly overdue. Don't hold your breath, since Mashatile is favourite to take over from winemaking Mbhazima Shilowa as premier.

Humour is really the only way to deal with it, and Greek jokes are much better than Roman ones. As Aristophanes said two-and-a-half millennia ago: 'Quickly, bring me a beaker of wine, so that I may wet my mind and say something clever.'

Appendix

THE SHAME IN NUMBERS

Statistical musings on the 2007 Chenin Challenge result.

Giving Martin Meinert his vote back, how safe is the Shameful victory and what does it tell us about the judges? The winner was selected by asking each judge to rank the eight finalists and the Shame was picked first by two judges, as compared to the FMC, which was favoured by only one judge. While ranking is a favourite method of selecting a winner in the case of a tie, why it was used in this case is surprising.

But perhaps even more surprising was that only two judges picked the winner, with three other wines getting a first place vote. Assuming the judges know what they're doing and vote honestly, if there was a clearly superior wine or a consistent style of Chenin sought by the judges, statistics would require more judges to choose it as favourite.

The way to see this requires a splash of common sense. We have eight wines and five judges. We can choose the two judges who agree out of the five in ten ways. These two judges can make eight different wine choices. Once they have chosen, the third judge can choose his or her favourite in seven ways, the fourth judge in six ways and the fifth judge in five ways, giving a total number of possible ways the result could have arisen as 10x8x7x6x5 = 16,800.

The total number of possible outcomes is 8x8x8x8x8 = 32,768, which gives the probability of the particular result we observed as 16,800/32,768 = 0.51. Which is certainly non-intuitive: if we select five wines at random out of eight, over half the time we expect to have exactly two coincident matches. For homework you can easily check that three coincidences happen 29 per cent of the time.

The Challenge result is thus consistent with the judges making their decisions *randomly*. Although of course the actual winning wine would have only one chance in eight of being the victor.

As Pinot Noir prophet Anthony Hamilton Russell remarked à propos competition results: 'Once technical faults are eliminated, the question of rating wines becomes an aesthetic one, with no "correct" answer.' The rankings of the Chenin Challenge judges confirm that the panel was far from unanimous – in fact, the same result could have been achieved by rolling five eight-sided dice. Adding up the scores would have been a fairer option, as it encodes how much a judge favours a wine rather than simply nominating a favourite, which throws the baby of personal preference out with the bathwater of statistics.

PLATTER'S MONKEYS

Some statistical musings on Platter's 2006 selection of five-star stunners

It's a statistical curiosity, even if an extremely unlikely one, that a team of monkeys sitting at a bank of typewriters could produce the collected works of William Shakespeare, given enough time. Which adds another suspect to the line-up of Christopher Marlowe, Francis Bacon and Edward de Vere, 17th Earl of Oxford, for Shakespeare conspiracy theorists searching for a replacement author for *As You Like It*.

So how would they fare at choosing five-star wines for the annual Platter's wine guide? About as well as the tasters who assembled in Stellenbosch.

One of their number, Cathy van Zyl, in her blog on the website www.grape.org.za, gives the facts of the matter: 72 wines proposed for five-star glory, 13 tasters with each voting for between 20 and 30 wines and success if seven or more pick the same wine.

Wine-tasting monkeys are easier to simulate on a computer than the real thing, and besides, zoos take a dim view of plying primates with alcohol, no matter how genetically similar to wine tasters, and even if monkeys are popular in some wine circles. (May-Eliane de Lencquesaing, chatelaine of Bordeaux super second Pichon Longueville Comtesse de Lalande, was inseparable from hers and would travel the world with it perched on her shoulder until quarantine regulations become too bothersome.)

Back at the PC, if our 13 computer monkeys choose on average 26 wines, then two-thirds of the time they will end up with between 9 and 13 five-star wines, with 11 the most likely outcome – which reproduces the verdict of Stellenbosch. If you told a Bayesian statistician that a monkey majority selected 11 wines, she would even be able to tell you the average number of wines chosen, fulfilling Van Zyl's prophecy: 'Some will criticise the process, citing statistical formulae as to why it is more difficult to get a majority vote when the class is large and the number of judges numerous than when the number of wines in the class is small and the judges fewer in number.'

While some would argue that such a small number of majority picks implies a lack of consistency between tasters rather than the selection of the 'best wines', rather than throw brickbats at the process, bunches of bananas are in order, as the monkeys are clearly on the right track when they can select the same number of five-star wines as a committee of experts. The next step will be to see if the primates pick the same wines.

Cathy called the tasting 'tremendous fun', which is reason enough for it to continue. But perhaps more useful than a list of five-star survivors, which tend to suffer from unexpected price rises and stock shortages as soon as their identities appear on a website, would be a list of nominees. Leading French wine writer Michel Bettane reckons that competition gold medals are a victory of compromise over character and hence it is better to seek silver, which typically had at least one champion. Applying the logic of Bettane, nominees are a better bet than winners, as for a team of monkeys to choose the same 72 wines from the 5,000 tasted for the guide, might take a while.

Index

K

Kabakov, Ilya 126
Kalashnikov, Mikhail 178
Kanonkop 70
Kent, Marc 68, 79, 102, 129, 155
Kentridge, William 48, 108, 124,
        124–129
King, Dave 30, 34, 36, 42, 125, 127
Kladstrup, Don and Petie 35
Klein Vondeling 28
Klimt, Gustav 130
Knysna Wynproe gilde 8
Koons, Jeff 114–116
Kovalyov 46, 48, 49, 53
Kruger, Jimmy 96
Kruger, Johan 110
Kumala 32
Kyoto 9

L

Labels 17, 18, 20, 25, 33, 39, 48, 66,
        86, 104, 111, 118, 124, 126,
        129, 146, 152, 159, 177
  back 152
  talking 146
Lambour, Karl 137
La Motte 41
Lanzerac 15, 16
Laroche, Michel 93
Latour 23, 25, 74, 130, 159
Laube, James 65
Laubser, Maggie 127
Lawrence Osborne 14, 81
Leipoldt, Louis 130
Lencquesaing, Madame May-Eliane
        de 34, 42, 97, 159, 183–184
Lindstrom, Martin 142–146
Lockshin, Larry 152
London Review of Books 13, 73, 148

London wine competitions 57–58
Loosen, Ernie 37, 38, 39

M

Maack, Lars 33
MacQuitty, Jane 67, 68, 91
Madame May. *See* Lencquesaing,
        Madame May-Eliane de
Madeira 25, 41
Magazines, ethics 59–61
Malherbe, Jeanne 105
Manhattan 138–141
Manti, Gaetano 59
Manuel, Trevor 178
  Manure 100, 102, 107. *See
        also* Preparation 500
Marco Pierre White 7
Marketing 137–163
  sensory 142–146
  to America 140–141
Marmion, Patrick 14
Marula 82
Mashatile, Paul 180
Mason, Jo 30
Maugham, Somerset 52
Maxwell, Kim 90
McCoy, Elin 50, 71
McInerney, Jay 8, 9, 176
McKenzie, James 110
Medieval Kyoto cuisine 9
Meerlust 19, 29, 42, 57, 80, 81, 90,
        94, 97, 128, 129, 138, 147, 148
Meinert, Martin 172
Melck, Ronnie 51
Michelangelo International Wine
        Awards 56, 57, 67
Moinnereau, Tony 97
Molesworth, James 57, 152
Mondovino 68, 175